Praise for The Fifth Way Series

"I'm extremely confident David Brisbin's latest book, *Daring to Think Again* will be read years from now as the embodiment of conventional wisdom on Christian thought. While contemporary critics may find him controversial, I doubt they will find him wrong. In exploring the implications of the surprisingly useful metaphor of aboriginal songlines—the Aborigines' unwritten, lyrical, extraordinarily accurate maps of their vast ancestral lands, Brisbin's point is that an historically informed understanding of Christ's daring message provides us with a reliable guide for the navigation of a life lived with the sure knowledge of God's love. Brisbin is a cheerful tour guide to this new landscape. Generous with memorable anecdotes and humorous stories, he leads us in his role as one of contemporary Christianity's most fearless, honest and objective authors."

John C. Drew, Ph.D.,
Author/Blogger: American Thinker, Breitbart.com, PJMedia, FrontPage Magazine, World News Daily.

"Reading *The Fifth Way* is like spending time with the author, Dave Brisbin, who has a gift of making simple the complicated religious mess we have collectively made of Christianity. He is a voice in the wilderness and a breath of fresh air. If you consider yourself a follower of Jesus, then *The Fifth Way* may help you discover the path your heart has long been seeking."

Chris Falson
Singer/Songwriter/Composer, Author: Planted by the Water–The Making of a Worship Leader

"We have arrived at a fascinating moment in history. At the same time religious institutions have developed a science of spiritual growth, Christians are discovering that is not what they want. Rather than be herded from one stage to another, believers are asking whether there is another way to walk with God that depends more on Spirit than structure and in practice is more organic than programmatic. Dave Brisbin's answer is 'Yes! There is The Fifth Way.' Of all the books in the Christian marketplace today why should you read this one? To renew your mind, refresh your heart, and restore your soul."

Chuck Smith, Jr.
Author and Spiritual Director for Reflexion–A Spiritual Community

"Dave Brisbin's *The Fifth Way* is intelligently poetic and masterfully crafted to shed light on a blue print for living *now* in alignment with original biblical intent. It supported me to deepen my personal relationship with Christ and reaffirm that my spiritual purpose is to be the love that *I am* in each moment of this day."

Richard Gibbs
Former NBA Basketball Player, Addiction Specialist

"Dave and I met briefly at year twenty in my Christian journey and now here we are again at year forty. Our lives have merged again at an important crossroads, not just for ourselves but for the entire global community. It is time to enquire after the 'road that leads to good' and, as a result, to find 'soulrest' that will provide us with the energy of Jesus Christ to finish our passage upstream against increasingly stress-filled times. Dave proposes a *Fifth Way*; for what it's worth, I think he's right."

Graham Kerr
Former media person (Galloping Gourmet), Author: 'Flash of Silver, the leap that changed my world'

"I hate to admit that I am not what you would call an avid reader. But when I met Dave Brisbin and our conversation came around to his book, just the way he talked about it made me want to get my hands on it. When I did, I didn't delay in reading the first chapter. I was hooked. But I didn't read it fast. It's not that type of book. I savored each chapter, set it down and let it sink in. I was anxious to read on to the next but I felt that what I was reading demanded time to think about it, maybe even to read it again before going on. Dave writes beautifully but more than that, he thinks beautifully. He draws the reader to take a journey with him to investigate how we have tried to know God, solve life's difficulties, and see if there is another way. And there is. I am so anxious to share this book with all of my friends and family."

Lindy Boone Michaelis
Singer, Daughter of Pat Boone, Author: Heaven Hears

"I'm just 30 pages into *The Fifth Way*, and I'm disappointed...I was looking for an editing job, for a profitable project. Instead, what I've found is some of the best writing I've *ever* read. I can't imagine giving any advice. I will continue to read because your intellect, perception, observations, and writing skills compel me to do so, but I can't imagine charging you for my time. I should pay you for allowing me to read this inspired manuscript."

Jerry Granckow
Book Editor, Author: In Search of the Silver Lining

"It's not often that one can say 'This book changed my life.' But this book changed my life. Where others either consciously or sub-consciously promote division in the name of God, Dave teaches unity and the importance of connection with God and *all* people, regardless of one's chosen faith. Unlearning suspect teachings of the past while coming to a deeper understanding about the true meaning of love, the importance of not judging those around us, and the value of being present in each moment has been a blessing that is hard to put into words. Because of Dave's book, I have a better understanding of who Jesus *really* was and what he was trying to teach us. I enthusiastically encourage you to begin your journey along *The Fifth Way*."

Doug Corbin
VP, Chief Development Officer, Children's Hospital OC Children's Foundation

DARING TO
THINK AGAIN

RESTORING JESUS' ORIGINAL CHALLENGE
TO THE FAITH WE THINK WE KNOW

DAVID BRISBIN

A Companion to

The Fifth Way
A Western Journey to the
Hebrew Heart of Jesus

Daring to Think Again
Restoring Jesus' Original Challenge to the Faith We Think We Know

A Companion to The Fifth Way: A Western Journey to the Hebrew Heart of Jesus

Published in the United States of America
theeffect
27124 Paseo Espada, Suite 801
San Juan Capistrano, CA 92675
www.theeffect.org

ISBN: 978-1-7923-1569-5

Cover photography: Dan Grinwis, Joshua Hoehne

Printed in the United States of America

For those who dare give themselves permission
to follow a different drummer.

Contents

Author's Note

One thing you lack:
Go and sell all you possess and give to the poor,
and you will have treasure in heaven;
and come, follow Me.

Mark 10:21-22

OVER HALF A CENTURY AGO, MARSHALL McCLUHAN FAMOUSLY said that "the medium is the message," by which he meant that the form of media we use is what really communicates...not the content hitched along for the ride.

Now, no self-respecting content creator wants to believe this is true, but even if McCluhan goes a bridge too far, there is no doubt that media works hand in glove with content to create meaning, and to pretend that it doesn't misses the impact of every message we send.

Which communicates loudest—the words or the actions and attitude of the speaker? When Francis of Assisi said that we should preach the gospel continually and use words when necessary, he's reminding us that message and messenger, content and container both have voices and must be consistent.

It didn't take long for me working full time as a pastor to question our use of church as the medium to convey an ancient, Hebrew message. As it has come to be practiced in the West, church often implies that we can somehow intellectually absorb, from neat air conditioned rows, a way of spiritual life birthed in the shadow of the desert mountain and lived out in the streets as a sweaty, messy, muscular journey to truth.

What is the real message being conveyed by our spiritual media today? This question has remained on the tip of my mind as I've worked to pour content into *this* medium: a book. *Another* book.

Centuries, or even just a few generations ago, there wouldn't have been such a concern that the printed word would distort the message of an ancient spirituality rooted in the land and its people. But today even the printed word has become less and less...printed, with any permanence. Ever-changing and merely virtual, words form projected "content" for screens of all shapes and sizes from which we consume only the most attractive information as fast as screens can refresh.

We have been conditioned to read less and skim more. We have conditioned our writers to write less and simplify more, to create the tag lines and infographics that will quickly soundbite information into twenty-first century attention spans. In such a frenetic, ADHD-inducing environment, how can a current, Western book become a partner, a faithful medium for a message challenging us to sell everything and follow a dusty, unassuming man along a path that unfolds only in real time—a primarily non-verbal medium that we will surely miss if we're moving any faster than a four-mile-an-hour walking pace?

The Way of Jesus is a classic hero's journey, a rite of passage that Carl Jung called an "almost perfect map of the soul." We live now as if we've outgrown spiritual maps, leaving formal rites of passage in our cultural dust along with even the memory of their importance to each of us. But without these markers of life transitions anchoring our day to day lives, we speed along, too fast to resonate with a man who spoke from a world that moved at such a deliberate pace.

It is no accident that Jesus never answered a question with a direct answer. Even when he was simply asked where he was going, his answer, "come and see," brought questioner and answer emphatically and wordlessly face to face. Speaking in parables and riddles, stories and metaphor, Jesus is breaking down our dependence on abstract concepts and engaging us to live our daily lives as medium for a message that can't be contained in words. We see him always working to make the voice of his medium and the voice of his message speak as one for those with "ears to hear."

I want to try to do the same.

If you are looking for quick answers to pressing questions, you may feel the shock of deceleration as we slow back down to walking pace. Each chapter is not presenting hard and fast answers as much as time to reconsider what you believe you're convinced of and to decide whether your beliefs are leading where you really want to go. In story, image, and metaphor, each chapter will certainly present a direction I've taken, but not so much to persuade as to offer alternative views to challenge common beliefs, our inherited "traditions" about Jesus' message and our daily lives.

Even so, this book is not a debate. To reduce Jesus's message to an argument over absolutes is to miss the unfolding hero's journey, the rite of passage that is an *embrace* of mystery and uncertainty, that doesn't try to resolve paradox even as it convinces us of truth—a truth that has the power to make us free only as we stop imploring it to remove the discomfort of uncertainty at the heart of life.

Engaging the *how* of Jesus' medium
before we consider the *what* of his message
is the challenge that must be accepted first.

How Jesus traveled, his medium, is the key to understanding the content of his message and not the other way around. We will never be able to follow where Jesus is ultimately leading unless we first see *how he traveled*: systematically clearing out anything standing in the way of his Way. To those still seeking eternal life—life that is eternally alive—Jesus' original challenge to sell everything and follow him is metaphor for the willingness to uproot everything we think we know that may stand in our way.

This is not a straightforward process. We don't know what stands in the way, so we must become willing to sell it all and descend into uncertainty for a time, just as Jesus did in the wilderness, in the grave, and over and over throughout his life. Jesus said *he* was the way, the medium...which means for Jesus, the medium is the message. Use words when necessary.

Here is an invitation to slow down, disconnect from other media, and walk the land for a time. Suspend your need for quick fixes and see what unfolds at four miles per hour. Begin the process of moving from the familiar to the uncertain and back again in the never-ending cycle, the rite of passage that Jesus called the "sign of Jonah" and the ancient church called the "paschal mystery," the descent before the ascent that both claimed is our only Way home to Father.

Introduction

When I realized I was not who I thought I was,
I was ready for a journey.
When I realized God was not who I thought he was,
the journey began.

HOW COULD I HAVE KNOWN THAT THE MAN BEHIND THE RETAIL
counter asking me to come hear him play guitar Tuesday night was
actually calling me to a completely new life? I'd only known him
for a few months, and only as a talking head and shoulders behind
the glass counter full of microphones and audio gear.

We were both guitarists and church music directors—we knew
that much about each other. But to this day I don't know what
made me accept his invitation. I was busy, had all the friends I
needed, Tuesdays were full, every third guy you meet plays guitar...
But I heard myself saying yes.

And that single word changed the better part of everything.

It is endlessly interesting and frustrating at the same time that you
only see the shape of your life in retrospect...not while it's happening, but after it has. Sometimes you recognize you're in a hinge
moment—a moment that swings your life into a completely new
trajectory—but most times you don't. Or can't. Such moments can be
indistinguishable from any other, cloaked in apparent insignificance.

How could I have known that saying yes, then and again a few
weeks later when he asked me to sit in with him, would place me in
front of an addiction recovery community, introducing me to those
who would become my best friends and partners for the next

fifteen years and counting? How could I have known that those two yeses were the unfelt push to a falling in love with a group of broken, imperfect people who became more church than church to me? People whose only remaining choice in the chaos—to be transparently who they were—made them finally capable of change? And how could I have known that I would come to identify with them so deeply that I became finally capable of change myself?

You never know going in, but whether recognized or not, every moment is infinitely significant. Pregnant. Locked and loaded with the possibility of immense change. Just the willingness to participate in a moment is life changing, and whether that moment carries us along in permanently new directions becomes less and less important the more we learn to immerse and participate in *all* our moments.

Every moment is seeded and should be treated with the respect it deserves.

The call to spiritual formation can be a moment like this...a casual invitation whose full size and shape hide far below the waterline. Or the moment can be as wrenching as a divorce or other significant loss, with the call not heard in the noisy events themselves, but in the spaces left unoccupied as the dust begins to settle. If we're willing to engage, or if the pain is at least great enough to displace our objections, the journey begins.

Every moment is seeded.

How could I have known that my divorce some thirty years ago would send me on a spiritual journey that would take me as far from Jesus as I could get before bringing me back again? And how could I have known that my engagement to be remarried would create a religious confrontation that would send me back out, searching for a Jesus who would redefine what it meant for me to be Christian?

Though I hadn't practiced the Catholicism of my youth for nearly fifteen years, since leaving the religious order I entered out of high school, the pain I hoped would end with my first marriage became a new kind of pain that forced me to confront the bare fact that I was not the man I thought I was—religiously, spiritually, relationally. With the mask pulled, what was left? Who was I now? Who had I always been when I thought I was someone else?

I had no vocabulary for what was happening at the time, but I was being called out on a hero's journey, a rite of passage that always begins with a wounding, a stripping away, a separation from everything we think we know. As the dust began to settle on my barely furnished studio apartment, there was very little left to distract from that call and my only remaining choice: to be transparently who I was and answer...or not. And I didn't answer for a time, but once sufficiently past the paralyzing depression, I began consciously searching for anything other than church that promised to make sense out of life. Occupying nearly all my free time and all my mental space, I moved from religious science and theosophy to Eastern philosophy and comparative religion with paranormal stops at lucid dreaming and astral projection, clairvoyance, remote viewing, pyramidology...

Several years later, a casual invitation from a coworker brought me back to Christianity—in an Evangelical setting: familiar and wildly different at the same time. But to a man crossing the desert, it was oasis, and I flowed gratefully into the group and too quickly into leadership positions in music and pastoral training. Like a child humming with finger-stopped ears, I shouldered past growing disturbance over doctrine and practice, letting new distractions mask the voice that was still calling.

But about three years in, when a relationship with a woman ultimately brought us to our pastor to ask if he would perform our wedding, how could I have known that he would say he couldn't marry us...that according to the Bible and Jesus' teaching, my divorce was unlawful, that our remarriage would constitute adultery, and in such a marriage I would not be eligible to continue in church leadership. I wondered exactly when they were planning to let me know all this: that some sins were unforgivable, that for me, full membership was always out of reach, that no matter how hard I tried, Jesus would never let me outrun my sins.

It was a Calvary moment.

A moment when Jesus—and everything I had been so carefully building and tending, trusting and depending—was killed right in front of me.

It was the moment all the unanswered and unexplored questions rose to meet the question still hanging in the air, and I realized that either God was not who I thought he was or he was not who my church thought he was. And I really needed to know which because if these were the positions of the church, then maybe I wasn't a Christian. And if they really did reflect the teaching of Jesus, then maybe I wasn't his follower after all.

I had always been very good at two things: running—staying busy and distracted—and leaving. I was very good at leaving when I could no longer run, when I was beginning to hear things for which I had no other response. In that moment, though, I resolved to do neither, but to stay and really listen for the first time. Jesus had always been handed to me, wrapped in Catholic or Evangelical paper; it was time to find out if he was neither or both—something else entirely, someone I could actually follow for the rest of my life.

To this day I don't know what made me say yes to that painful invitation from life. Except maybe that when I realized I was not who I thought I was, I was ready for a journey, and when I realized God was not who I thought he was, the journey began.

So I heard myself saying yes, and that single word has changed absolutely everything.

I had no vocabulary for it then, but I was learning that the way to Pentecost always begins at Calvary. Or in non-religious terms, the way to the heights we crave always begins at the depths we fear. Life is so noisy, so full of shiny objects, we can play at the surface of things for a very long time. That deeper voice is always there, inviting, but our ability to say yes is only as good as our ability to cut through the noise and distraction that mask the significance of each moment.

The Calvary moment is the moment our distractions die.

It's always painful because for distractions to be good at their jobs, they can't look like distractions. They look like life itself, beautiful and necessary. But as we begin to identify with them and cling to them so fully that we no longer hear the deeper call, Jesus is standing there telling us that unless we hate our fathers and mothers, our family, and even our own lives, we won't be able to go where he's going. (Luke 14:26) And though the word *hate* in his native Aramaic language, *sena*, here means just to prefer less, his meaning is still radically clear, especially in a first century Hebrew culture where family and tribe meant survival itself. To be unwilling or unable to see past everything on which our culture and life experience has taught us to rely is to miss a deeper truth completely free of all visible means of support.

When a rich young man asks Jesus what he must do to find eternal life, though Jesus loves him for his obvious sincerity and desire to answer the call, he ultimately tells him the thing he still lacks is to sell everything he has and give it to the poor. If we're not careful, we will literalize and hear Jesus' challenge only in terms of material wealth. But four centuries later, an Egyptian monk named Serapion dug much deeper when he "sold the Book that told me to sell everything and give to the poor." To come to realize that even the expression of our own deeply held beliefs can stand between us and the truth we seek is to emerge at the trailhead of Jesus' Way.

Jesus recognized that he himself, his physical presence had become a distraction to his followers when he told them it was to their advantage that he have his Calvary moment and be physically removed so the Helper could come. And though in his idiomatic way of speaking it sounds like a passive handoff, he's telling us that the moment we release the last thing to which we're clinging—even our image of himself—is the real beginning...undistracted, we can finally see the unseen Help that was always there and choose to engage.

This is Jesus' original challenge...

He is challenging us to become willing to sell everything we think we know and everything we grasp for support. Everything. Even our own image of God and beliefs about the Book that gave us that image in the first place. To see distractions for what they are and prefer them less.

Before we can travel the Way of Jesus, we need to find our way to the Way. Jesus' challenge clears out anything that would stand in the way of his Way.

You may have already hit a Calvary moment, maybe several of them—traumatic or disturbing events, losses that pull back the familiar curtain to expose a reality you have no idea how to navigate. Or maybe there's just a growing sense of dissatisfaction that unsettles the peaceful landscape from time to time like small tremors along a fault line signaling much more activity beneath.

As Westerners, we have a very powerful system of belief, a collective philosophy and worldview that directs us across the landscape of our lives just as the ancient oral traditions, the chanted *songlines* of Australia's Aborigines have directed them across the terrain of the outback for thousands, perhaps even tens of thousands of years. But where the Aborigines consciously practice, preserve, and *update* their songlines to keep them grounded in the physical shape of the land and the realities of each new generation—deliberately singing them to navigate both their physical and spiritual worlds, we are most often unaware of how our Western songlines, our deeply set beliefs, affect our choices and attitudes.

In a chaotic, postmodern culture that is freefalling toward complete detachment from the grounding of the land and the guidance of our own ancient spirituality, a longing for renewed inner experience is growing. And just as I did, more and more of us are coming to the conclusion that we need to leave Jesus in order to pursue an authentic spiritual journey. Been there, done that: we see Jesus inextricably tied to an archaic, even superstitious system that has no power to take us anywhere we haven't already been. But we haven't been playing fair. We have remodeled and reshaped Jesus over centuries to fit Western culture, only to leave him now when he fails to deliver us out that culture's grasp.

We will never need to leave Jesus to find authentic spirituality.

We do need to become entirely ready to leave the Jesus we think we know, but that's not the same thing. Any authentic spiritual journey will always affirm the truth in the voice of the authentic,

Hebrew Jesus—a voice we can hear only if we accept Jesus' original challenge to sell everything first.

When we realize that we want to go somewhere we've never been before, somewhere off the familiar edge of our maps, we first have to become willing to question our Western songlines, our conscious or unconscious traditional beliefs. Truth is, we don't see the land around us, reality, directly; we see it only through the filter of our beliefs. Our beliefs limit the land we see to the land we think we know, and if we want to go somewhere else, we first have to see the possibility that it exists, which means selling the filter.

This authentic Hebrew Jesus—we will call him by his Hebrew name, *Yeshua*, to remind us that he will always be standing outside our set beliefs, challenging them—lived and expressed the only way to new landscapes, to Kingdom and Father. He is saying that wherever we are, the journey begins by being willing to nail our deepest traditions and rituals to a tree and see what may be left.

It wasn't until I was ready to leave Jesus entirely that I was entirely ready to see *Yeshua* as he really is and find that I was a fervent follower after all.

Picking up this book may have been a hinge moment. Of all the books you've handled, this one must seem no different, insignificant, even. You never know going in, but saying yes to questioning the deepest things you think you know and considering new ways of looking at what you thought was settled debate, is the beginning of a journey that will require everything you think is yours in exchange for changing everything.

No book is the answer itself.

But a good book always presents at least one new challenge, a new songline that when learned by heart, reveals its significance and allows us to see past our maps and simply walk the land.

Rites of Passage

A hero is not the one who completes the journey,
but the one whom the journey completes.

There is a war going on inside us.
And among us.

IT'S A WAR FOR OUR ATTENTION, A WAR TO ESTABLISH WHAT WE SEE
as meaningful in our lives, what we will pursue with the time we are
allotted and resources we've accrued. The weapons arrayed against
us are the torrent of voices inside our own minds and the noise of
those around us in person and media that draw us in a predictable
direction. Always toward the *whats* of life, the endless details and
distracting needs that drive us through moments rendered insignificant by a focus on outcomes we imagine always lie somewhere
other than wherever we are.

Most of us aren't aware of this war. Like riding a hot air balloon
pushed by the wind in the same direction at the same speed, the air
feels perfectly still; as we ride the torrent of voices—traveling same
direction and speed—it seems that life as lived in the torrent is all the
reality there is.

But there's another voice...

It doesn't actually speak, at least not like the others. In fact we can only hear it when we step *away* from the others. This voice is unassuming, never calls attention to itself or demands a thing. It just offers a silent possibility that Yeshua called *sherara*, truth in Aramaic, but with layers of meaning including that which liberates and opens possibility of harmonious direction—the true possibility of a very different way of living life that directly addresses our missing pieces and wages our war of meaning in a way we'd never anticipate in the midst of the torrent.

The irony is, we can never gain a foothold in this war as warriors. The aggressive-defensive, ever-strategic mindset of the warrior itself is the contradiction, the signature of surrender: we can only turn the tide of our attention toward true meaning and purpose as we mentally beat our swords into plowshares, become virtual gardeners. By changing the rules of engagement from hyperactive fear to a patient flowing with the rhythms of wind and weather, there is a slowing down, a mindful awareness of timeless landscape and life normally left unseen beneath the surface of things.

> Books are nothing more than words.
> Words have value; what is of value in words is meaning.
> Meaning has something it is pursuing, but the thing that it is pursuing cannot be put into words and handed down.
> *Chuang Tzu*

As the torrent of voices keeps us focused on the *whats* of life, the silent voice describes the *how*, the manner in which we proceed to true meaning—the only possibility of the contentment and conviction we all need as humans whether we know we want them or not. And this *how*, this manner of proceeding can't be transferred from one human to another; it can't be taught with words or diagrams. It can only be experienced and internalized in a journey that has been described as the hero's journey, a *rite of passage*.

The problem for us as modern Westerners is that we have no rites of passage left in our culture, so we don't know what it means or feels like to make significant life transitions or have them recognized and celebrated in the community. Dictionary-defined as a *ceremony or celebration that marks the transition from one phase of life to another*, we talk casually about a baby's first tooth or a child's first haircut being a rite of passage, a bar mitzvoth or debutante ball. But though these events are milestones in life, they don't provide the three essential components of a true rite of passage: *separation, transition, and re-incorporation*.

Looked at this way, ceremony and celebration are not really big enough words to encompass all that a rite of passage is. A wedding is a ceremony and celebration, but as a daylong event, is not a rite of passage, whereas divorce is not necessarily a ceremony and not usually a celebration, but almost always a rite of passage because it forces a journey through the three phases of separation, transition, and re-incorporation...and of course, because it contains pain. There is no hero's journey without a wounding and no rite of passage without the pain of separation and risk of transition that precedes the joy of re-incorporation.

Ceremonies can mark each of the three phases of a true rite of passage, but it's the journey through each phase that creates the awareness of change, both for the hero and his or her community. All ancient cultures and current aboriginal ones had and have rites of passage built into their communal lives. At the age of twelve or thirteen, girls leave their families to become wives and mothers, and boys are taken by the men for a painful and usually risky journey that when completed will mark their entry into manhood. We in the modern West need to relearn the importance of the journey from familiar security to wilderness and back again.

⊙ ⊙ ⊕ ⊕ ⊕

Aboriginal people do not believe they end at their skin or finger-
tips. The earth as mother is real to them, and their history, culture
and purpose are embodied in the land.

David Suzuki

Like most of us, I'd heard of a walkabout long before learning to
appreciate its deep significance...

Walkabout is the rite of passage for young boys of Australia's
Aborigines—often cited as the oldest continuous culture on earth.
For some forty thousand to sixty thousand years, bridging the end
of the last ice age some twelve thousand years ago, these people
have flourished as nomadic hunter gatherers. Perhaps because of
the harshness of the land, they never began farming and herding,
never settled into cities or built great stone monuments and buildings, but like a blind man who develops a greater sense of hearing
or smell, it seems that the Aborigines built a heightened interior
culture that was portable, that could be securely carried along as
they followed the seasons and sources of food.

They developed a sophisticated cultural and spiritual system of
belief, never written down, but carried from generation to generation
embedded in song and dance and ritual tied intimately to the land
that gave them life. This system and these beliefs revolve around
oneness with creation and nature, and in their eyes, are written *there*—
in landscape and landmark—just as surely as we have written our
systems and beliefs in books. Their shape shifting creator beings,
sometimes human, sometimes animal, moved through the land
creating and shaping it with their tracks of passage in the time of the
"dreaming" or "dreamtime," a timeless time, an all-at-once *everywhen*
that for the Aborigines constitutes the absolute, objective reality of
the universe—not the linear sequence of events we experience each
day.

The tracks of the creator beings, *dreaming tracks,* are still visible on the land: large depressions are footprints or seatprints, ridges, rocks, outcroppings and caves may be resting body shapes or details of events along a storyline, and a traveler can follow the tracks through the land if he knows the details of the dreaming. And these portable stories, woven into song and dance were carried and recited and sung each and every day until the people *became the songs* themselves and, responsible for keeping them alive, passed them on to each new generation as their birthright, their life sustaining map through their world, their portal between dreamtime and linear time sung by countless generations all connected with each other across time and space...all at once and everywhen.

The songs transported them into dreamtime around their fires at night and led them through the physical dreaming tracks by day, and if the people kept the songs alive, the songs would keep the people alive.

They were their *songlines.*

The totality of what songlines are and how they work is very difficult for Western minds to grasp, but for our purposes, Aboriginal songlines are the oral archives of an entire culture set to rhythm and chant. Charting the creation of land and sea, melodic contours mirror the shape of the land, and rhythm can describe the movement of different types of animals, while language embeds descriptions of land formations, plant remedies, hunting fields, or location of water. In a culture that doesn't build or write or settle in cities surrounded by farms, that forever walks the land, their songlines were living maps and guides that ensured their survival.

The Westerners who colonized Australia in the late eighteenth century were astonished that Aborigines could navigate hundreds and thousands of kilometers of bush without the aid of any instrumentation or written direction. By physically singing the song corresponding to the area being traveled, performing rituals at each sacred site within that sung track, the people could read the land unerringly and follow the dreaming tracks even through the deserts of Australia's interior. The entire continent is covered by an extensive network of songlines some extending only a few kilometers, others hundreds of kilometers through lands of different tribes, languages, and cultures. By stitching together the songlines of different tribes, journeys can continue without language being a barrier as the melody and rhythm of a song describes the shape of the land as much as the words themselves. The shape of the song to be sung is literally the analog of the shape of the land to be traveled.

When an Aborigine boy reaches the age of twelve or thirteen, he is taken by the men away from the company of women and children and out into the bush: *separation*. From there, he must go walkabout—alone on the land for up to six months, following the songlines he has been rehearsing his entire life as his only guide: *transition*. In his walkabout, the boy must be able to make his own shelters and find food and water. In addition to reading the land, he must know how to hunt and trap, which plants are safe to eat and which can heal wounds. He must be able to defend himself and live his relationship with the land through a journey that may carry him over a thousand kilometers.

But as well as surviving physically, he must use his songlines to enter the all at once experience of dreamtime, live the deep connection between himself and the land and all the generations before him who lived connected to the land. The harsh challenges and real risk of the physical walkabout mixed with the deep spiritual experience of timeless time proves the boy's transition from boyhood to manhood both to the community without and to the boy himself within. When he returns, he is celebrated in the community as now taking his place among the men of the tribe: *re-incorporation*. There is no doubt in anyone's mind who he is and what purpose he serves in the tribe.

It may come as a shock to many of us in the West that the shape of this journey is exactly the same as that of Yeshua leaving the security of his family and livelihood to go walkabout in the wilderness before coming home again to teach with an authority that astonished. And as Yeshua invites us to follow this same shape of his Way, he's saying that conviction, assurance, and acceptance like this can't be bought at any price, and only comes as a result of the pain of separation, the challenge of transition, and the joy of re-incorporation.

☉ ☽ ⊕ ⊕ ⊕

> Myth is stories about the way things never were,
> but always are.
>
> *Marcus Borg*

Are the songlines true?

This would be one of the first questions we would ask as modern Westerners before compulsively dismissing them when they don't pass the tests our worldview demands. Immersed in the torrent of voices that demand accuracy and certainty before acceptance, we tend to instinctively ask the wrong questions of a spiritual tradition, including our own.

Songlines, like all spiritual traditions, run deep beneath the ever changing details at the surface of life, vibrating at the center of things, at the level of unchanging bedrock where they can always be true even if not accurate. They are true because they can inerrantly guide us through the details, take us hundreds of kilometers through hostile terrain by recalling landmarks that never change regardless of changing circumstance, emotion, or trauma. The landmarks set down by the gods themselves in these creation stories mirror the bedrock milestones of a spiritual journey to reconnection, and so the songs that describe them are always true and always relevant, always pointing in the direction we really want to go whether we know it or not.

As a culture that builds and writes and settles in great cities surrounded by farms and connected by superhighways, but never walks the unpaved land, we have not only lost the map that traces our journey, we have forgotten there ever was such a map at all. Instead of living a heritage with a memory sixty thousand years long, we live in a world only five hundred years in the making, a heritage forged in Europe's Enlightenment when science and reason replaced mythic songlines as the true description of our journey. As a people divorced from the land and the songs that connect inner and outer landscape, the stories we tell ourselves are only as true to us as they are accurate. They reside as we do on the surface of things, accurately describing details, but lacking the power to transport us to the timeless center, the all at once everywhen where truth has no need of factual accuracy.

From Richard Rohr:

When the single image morphs into a universal image, you get its archetypal significance, and as the prophet Zechariah says, "You will weep for him as you would weep for your only child, you will mourn for him as if he is every child" (Zechariah 12:10). That is how images can transform us, but only if we can move beyond the mere literal, specific image to the universal and always true image. Fundamentalists find this very hard to do; mystics and great poets seem to be able to do nothing else. Mystics wait for experiential knowledge of the Divine and are not satisfied with mere memorized answers.

The most important questions in life don't have answers.
Only the experience of asking.

There is no answer to life. There is only the experience of living. But life is difficult, and in our fear we have tried to reduce life in the West to a risk-free equation that will render the sum of our salvation. And though we may fool our heads, we never fool our hearts, and beneath the math, we know something is wrong. Something is missing. But as a mystery-and-risk-averse people, it is very difficult for us to believe that anything as improbable as a songline could ever hold the key to that something.

What is the goal of a spiritual journey? At the bottom of a dog-pile of answers, it is a *freedom from fear* that only comes from knowing who we really are—the fearless freedom of knowing our place, that we *have* a place with all that truly is. To return where we started, leaving no doubt in anyone's mind who we are and what purpose we serve in the tribe is a conviction, an assurance, and an acceptance that can't be bought at any price, and only comes as a result of the pain of separation, the challenge of transition, and the joy of re-incorporation.

The spiritual journey is a hero's journey, a rite of passage that can't be taught or learned, only traveled. If we think we know the way, imagine it all laid out in our minds, we've lost the way before we begin.

Those of us who have tried to wheedle explicit answers out of Yeshua have always been disappointed. The thought of a journey to an unseen Father without a physical Yeshua to grasp was too much for Thomas and Philip at John 14. Thomas: "We don't know where you are going, how can we know the way?" Yeshua: "I am the way and the truth and the life and no one comes to the Father but through me." Philip: "Show us the Father and that will be enough for us." Yeshua: "He who has seen me has seen the Father; how can you say, show us the Father?"

The path to unseen Father must be paved with unseen stones.

The way to an unseen God must also be unseen. A visible path can only lead to a visible god, a defined image we call idol. The Way of Yeshua is a true rite of passage, a hero's journey. It's not what we think it will be. It never is. It's not what we think it is, and it's not what we think at all. It is the pure experience of the pain of being separated from everything we think we know and everything we think we are. It's the turmoil of the challenge of identity faced in the transition between worlds—no longer a part of the old world and not yet understanding the way of the new—and the assurance of returning changed, identified, purposeful. The Way takes on a life of its own, and we can't know the Way until we travel the Way, but we do have guides if we will trust them: ancient and contemporary people and stories pointing toward what is always true.

Though we don't have songlines in the West occupying a place in our culture that the songlines of the Aborigines do in theirs, we do have Scripture and stories about life, meaning, and spirituality that predate or transcend our five hundred years of enlightenment. Sacred stories that were told by people of both East and West who saw footprints in the land we no longer entertain. Do we know where they are actually pointing?

What are those stories really telling us? And are we true to the telling or do we just believe we know them because we've heard them recited our entire lives through the filter of a worldview completely alien to the time of the telling?

We've been told how to believe and what to believe first by parents and schools, churches and creeds; then as our worlds expand, by media and government, religion and philosophy—mere immersion in our culture. And immersed in a culture obsessed with accuracy, truth is rarely considered. To whichever landscapes our Scripture and stories may have originally pointed, it's now our belief *about them* that shapes the land we see rather than the land itself shaping *us*, saving us from walking in circles of our own creation. How can we know whether we're walking the land as God shaped it or just as we imagine we understand? The answer, of course, will not be rational, but if the directions we walk and the destinations we experience leave us fearful and unidentified, unconvinced of our own acceptance, knowing that something is missing, something is wrong, then it seems we need permission to rethink the stories that give shape to our faith and find older songs to sing.

The audacity it takes to give ourselves permission to think unorthodox thoughts, sand our lumber against the grain, is beyond many if not most of us. Yeshua understood the power of long standing tradition and authority in his own culture, and right at the beginning of the Sermon on the Mount—and we can imagine possibly at the beginning of every teaching—he not only gives the people permission to rethink their traditional beliefs, he shows them exactly how it works. Sometimes called the *Six Antitheses*, Yeshua redefines the intent and purpose of the Law using the formula: "You have heard it was said to those of old... (*tradition*), but I say to you... (*challenge*)." Yeshua states the traditional beliefs about six issues that he knows are keeping the people from intimate connection with God and each other, then challenges them with new songlines that map a part of the way he has traveled himself.

This is exactly how it works: overcoming the fear of separating from familiar but limiting *traditions* and *challenging* them in order to follow archetypal *songlines* through unfamiliar spiritual landscapes as a transition toward reincorporation into deeper community.

An interior rite of passage.

Near the end of the Sermon, Yeshua acknowledges how hard it is to break with the authority of traditional beliefs and follow an uncertain, *unwritten* path saying that the way to life is narrow and the gate to the way is constricted and few go there... He's saying that if we're not aware, the torrent of cultural and religious voices pulls us along creating its own reality as it goes. But if we can grab hold of a rock or a branch near the banks of the current for just a moment, we will feel the presence of that other voice, hear it singing a timeless song.

There are big questions in life. They point to our deepest, most human concerns. These questions don't have answers as we think of answers in a rational sense, but like landmarks in the distance, point us in experiential directions. Are we brave enough, or just tired and hurt enough to dare challenge what we think we know about such questions in order to see where a new songline may lead?

Maybe we could start with twelve... Take twelve big issues and ask how we should be navigating these landmarks and the questions scattered around them like alluvial rocks: question what we really believe about *love, law, engagement, interpretation, inspiration, vulnerability, fear, trust, presence, contentment, destiny, release.* Twelve issues, twelve opportunities to accept Yeshua's original challenge to sell all we possess and follow him—not what we have come to *believe about* him, but having sold that book as well, follow the true shape of his journey, a shape that will guide us along a topography that we may see again for the very first time.

It is no accident there are twelve. In the symbolism of ancient Hebrew numbers, three is the number of completion and four is the number of the earth. Three times four makes twelve the number of the fulfilment of earthly systems, government and leadership and community. Where you see twelve tribes or twelve apostles or the twelveness of every measurement of the New Jerusalem, you are seeing this number purposely conveying what is true regardless of whether it is accurate. It's the number of a complete cycle, the journey of the earth, the land, through the twelve lunar cycles of the year or the twelve constellations of the zodiac. A setting off and a return to where we began; it's a hero's journey, a rite of passage.

This is where we need to go, where we really want to go if we're willing to look beyond the fear of the pain of separation. Let's go walkabout, engage the hero's journey, move into the disturbance of the big questions, challenge what we think we believe, enter liminal space and give ourselves permission to follow the contour of the land wherever rhythm and melody may lead.

THE CHALLENGES

THE SHAPE OF THE WAY

TRADITION
*God created us to love him back;
the more we love, the more God loves us.*

You Had Me at Hello

LOVE

Happy families are all alike;
every unhappy family is unhappy in its own way.
Leo Tolstoy, Anna Karenina

There is a sameness to love.

IF THIS SEEMS COUNTERINTUITIVE, IF IT SEEMS THAT LOVE AND sameness don't belong in a sentence together, it may be because love certainly doesn't *feel* the same in all its roles and variations. From husband and wife or parent and child to a close friendship, a platonic or spiritual relationship, or a good Samaritan caring for a complete stranger, the experience of love can be as far as the east is from west as we feel engulfing passion, warm affection, or nothing at all. We might even feel an active dislike or disgust as we continue to do the loving thing, the best we can, for someone who inspires no warmth in us whatsoever.

But feelings are misleading because they have only to do with what we are getting *out* of a particular relationship, not what we are putting in. And if it's really love that we are putting in, there will be a sameness in the quality of our relationships regardless of how we feel about them...the *effect* of love is always the same.

That's why Tolstoy was right, that happy families are all alike: happy families are defined by their love for each other, and love creates predictable circumstances, environments, and atmosphere. Happy families may all look very different at first glance, and family members can feel different about each other in the process of being happy, but they all have certain traits in common—trust, respect, loyalty, affection, and whatever level of civility is culturally agreeable. When you walk into their homes, you feel the spirit of the place—the safeness, the warmth, the ease and sense of connection. It is a place you want to be and to which you want to return.

Unhappy families and unhappy relationships are all unhappy in their own way because they are not defined by love, which is universal in its effect, but by fear and the circumstances of their pain, which are unique to each. Unhappy families are unhappy because at least one member is hurting so badly that his or her pain becomes the center of gravity around which everyone else revolves. And the acting out of that pain, the abuse it creates, hurts everyone near, until eventually everyone is in pain, creating new centers of hurtful gravity.

Some of us have been hurting so long, have been defined by our pain or the pain of others for so long, that we don't even know who we are apart from it anymore. The film *Moscow on the Hudson* captures this perfectly as it tells the story of a Russian musician who defects to the United States from the old Soviet Union, taking up residence in New York City. In the moment of his defection, all the circumstances of his life are suddenly changed, and with them, everything that he'd come to see as himself is changed as well. As he's struggling to transition into his newfound life and freedom, he tries to explain the difficulty: "When I was in Russia, I did not love my life...I loved my misery. You know why? Because it was *my* misery. I could hold it. I could caress it. I loved my misery."

He loved his misery because it was the one thing he could always count on. Anything he valued in life had been taken from him, could always be taken from him at any moment—but whatever was taken, whatever happened, his misery remained. It was constant; it would never leave or forsake him. It belonged to him alone, so he came to belong to it, to fully give himself over to the one thing in life he knew could not be taken without his permission. Then suddenly, in a moment, it was gone. Or at least many of the reasons for it were gone. What to do? How to react when the four walls of his tiny cell were suddenly removed, and everything that had made him who he was, was no longer present?

He had two choices; we all do. We can change our image of ourselves to reflect reality, or we can try to change reality to reflect the image of who we think we are.

How many people do we know who live their lives in a constant state of chaos, of "drama?" When the law of averages, if nothing else, would seem sure to come to their rescue, these people defy the odds and continue to move from crisis to crisis in a steady stream, actually creating new crises when life fails to serve them up. How many times do we hear of people physically cutting themselves just to feel the pain that reminds them they are still alive? How many take drugs, drink alcohol, engage in all manner of extreme behavior and even extreme sports to hold off the relentless onslaught of reality-as-it-is by desperately trying to preserve image-as-it-is.

Sometimes the process is subtler: there are those who have simply learned to expect the worst, to expect Murphy's Law to come kicking down their doors at any moment, that if something seems too good to be true, it certainly is. The cynics, the skeptics, the pessimists and fatalists among us have been programmed by pain to expect more of the same, and what they come to expect, they can begin to create in self-fulfilling prophecy. When any of us begin to see ourselves in terms of our pain, pain becomes who we are, and we guard it as fiercely as we guard our own lives.

There's also a powerful sense of individuality and uniqueness in angst and pain—it sets us apart from the crowd in a way the sameness of love does not. Almost every teenager believes that no one has ever gone through what they are going through, that no one understands, that no one has ever felt their pain. And if the narcissism of youth becomes solidified in adulthood, then pain, personality, and personhood become fused; there is no longer distinction between them.

Culturally, the icon of the tough, unsmiling, tortured loner with an unspeakable but fascinating past, wandering from town to town, righting perceived wrongs but never forming permanent attachments, has become the ubiquitous fantasy hero. But from Shane to Bond to Batman, the fascination lasts only as long as the pain that drives them in and out of our lives. We want them because we know we can't have them: to smile, to settle down, is to break the spell, to become domesticated, neutered, and as dull as our culture's view of the family man or woman framed in the doorway of tract homes full of furniture and noisy children.

The sameness of love, the predictable qualities it creates in people and their relationships, actually becomes an object of derision, an imagined loss of individuality and power, a bore, an intolerable, sterile existence. We cling to the uniqueness of our pain and resist sameness, because we fear being lost in the crowd, becoming one of many, one with many, unspectacular without any distinguishing features that are ours alone. Better to survive on an island of pain that is ours alone than to drown in a sea of sameness from any other source. Or as Satan declares in Milton's *Paradise Lost*, "It is better to rule in Hell than serve in Heaven." If we're honest, we admire that at some level, or at least we understand.

We resist the sameness of a love so powerful that it levels us all—removing our imagined identities, our individual and unique notions of ourselves and replacing them with the identity, the predictable and universal qualities of its Source. At the same time, we are drawn to a love like this. Like moths to a flame, we long for it as the deepest expression of who we really are as humans.

Jerry McGuire, the title character of the movie, is a fictional personification of the tug of war we all face as we live between the cultivation of personal distinction and the sameness of perfect love.

Jerry is young, beautiful, successful in a glamorous business, and ultimately empty. Having lost any sense of who he is apart from all that has become his life, he tries to redefine himself in a memo, a manifesto that when made public, ends his job and starts his journey. But Jerry, like all of us, doesn't change overnight. He immediately doubts the reality of the deep stirrings that changed his course, and in fear, returns to his old ways. He tries to run his new life and business as he did the old ones, but this time he has one thing going for him that he didn't have before—a living example of love.

The one employee who sticks with him is a single mother with whom Jerry becomes involved and then marries. We watch as Jerry is both drawn toward and repulsed by the realities of instant fatherhood, hearth, and home—always being pulled away by the demands and allure of the business he's struggling to rebuild. Realizing she's on the losing side of this battle, his wife reluctantly separates from him, going to live with her sister. But in textbook fashion, Jerry, like all of us, soldiers on even as everything is being stripped away: all his options, his business, dreams, wife, even the son he was just getting to know are gone before he's willing to take an unthinkable risk—to see whether love beyond anything he's ever experienced really exists.

He races to his sister-in-law's house—mentally rehearsing everything he's going to say to his wife—sweating, intense, terrified of how she might react and what she might say. In a comical moment across a living room full of single women, he catches sight of his wife as she enters, and after a breath begins his impassioned monologue telling her everything he rehearsed in his mind, everything he hopes will convince her to come back to him, to love him again, to put their home together again. It's as if he's trying to cast a spell, weaving his words continuously, layer upon layer, until she mercifully stops him almost in mid-sentence saying,

"Shut up. Just shut up...you had me at hello."

What Jerry didn't understand, couldn't understand, was that there never was a time when his wife had stopped loving him. That for her, not loving him was not ever an option. She loved him despite her own best interests, and her love wasn't based on anything rational; it certainly wasn't based on his behavior. She loved him, and though she realized she couldn't live with him, that there was nothing in him on which to hang a relationship, the love never stopped or altered or dimmed. All he had to do was turn and face it again, and it was right there...at hello.

How could he have known? How could he have expected such a love existed for him? He'd never seen it, never experienced it, didn't deserve it, but there it was. The painful process of rebirth that began with disorientation and disillusionment and loss became completed in the reality of a love that had always seemed much too good to be true.

But here is where any analogy to God's love begins to break down. The best of human love, even if unconditional, is still graduated and exclusive: it has degrees of intensity and is focused on some but not others. This is as far as most of us are ready, willing, or able to take our concept of perfect love, but it is right at this point that such a love as God's has only just begun to shock us.

In response to the Sadducees absurd question at Matthew 22, Yeshua says that no one will marry or be given in marriage in the next life but "are like the angels in heaven." He is making an incredible statement—a frightening one. To have no exclusive relationships, no wife or husband holding us at night; to belong to no one in particular but everyone in general; to have no best friend or confidant or lover who is exclusively ours and keeps our deepest secrets; to have *no secrets*... The thought alone is disorienting and disturbing, but ultimately, it's terrifying. Our lives without such close and exclusive relationships would be as alien an existence to us as the aboriginal Moken people of Indonesia who, with no words in their language for "want," "when," "hello," or "goodbye," live without even the concepts of elapsed time and personal possession—as one organism with separate bodies. It feels less than fully human to even imagine a life without time and possessions, without levels of affection and trust, without an inner circle of just a few or just one.

Yeshua is telling us that his Father's love is so powerful it obliterates our imagined individuality and uniqueness, so complete, so fulfilling, that it even extinguishes any need for the exclusive relationships that are the basis of human life as we know it. How can we attempt to conceptualize such a love? We all have favorites; as finite humans, we have to. It's much easier to believe in a God who has favorites too, even if it means we may not be one of them. Somehow it seems easier to bear a familiar pain we understand than accept an alien joy we don't—and if we can't rise to a level where we can accept such a consummate love, we bring the love down to a level we can.

A friend told me about a church service he attended where a pastor was moving down a line of people, laying hands on them and giving a "prophetic word from the Lord" to each in succession. When he reached one particular person, a man blind from birth, he stopped in his tracks as if jolted by an electrical shock and exclaimed, "The Lord *really* loves you." My friend thought this was a wonderful testament to how much God loved this man, but I was thinking, "As opposed to what?" To the person right before him, or after him, whom he loved less? How were those others made to feel, standing right next to the man God "really" loved? What are we saying to each other when we say such things? That there are degrees to God's love? That some of us are loved more or less? How can that be in the face of everything Yeshua said and did, and how can such a statement possibly be a "word from the Lord?"

We speak about King David being "beloved" by God, as the Scriptures record, as if he had been God's favorite; as if God loved David more than or in a way different than anyone else; as if being God's "beloved" has anything to do with a special action from God at all. David wasn't God's beloved because God loved him any more or differently than any other person who has ever walked this planet...David was God's beloved because he lived his life *as if* he were God's beloved, because he came to understand what God's love really meant, and simply turned to face it.

Put a lamp on a table and plug it into a 110-volt socket in the wall. Screw in a 15-watt bulb and softly light up the room. Take it out and put in a 100-watt bulb and squint against the glare. What happened? It's the same 110 volts, the same fixture...did the wall socket *really* love the 100-watt bulb?

The Source is always the same; it's the wattage of the receiver that makes the difference. This is what that pastor felt when he laid his hands on the blind man—not a special love for him from God, but a special reflection of that love in the life of the man himself. God's love is the same everywhere and in every direction, but we all absorb and reflect it to different degrees: the love is the same; our acceptance is different. The language we use betrays the concepts we hold—ideas that bar us from approaching the radical conclusion of God's unchanging love and skew our understanding of the Scriptures that describe this love.

Think of how we understand the famous verse at John 3:16, "For God so loved the world, that he gave his only begotten son, that whoever believes in him shall not perish, but have eternal life." Buried in this verse is that tiny word, "so." "For God *so* loved..." How do we typically understand the word "so?" "It all happened so fast." "He was so mad." "I love you so...much." We use the word "so" in contemporary English to express degree or quantity—the "much" is always implied. It's like the old Johnny Carson routine where he'd begin a joke by saying, "It was *so* hot today..." and the audience would respond in unison: "How hot was it?" "For God so loved..." and we automatically respond, "How much does he really?" But there's no how much or how far or how high with respect to God. Measurement has no meaning next to an infinite God and his love.

Anything that can't be measured always looks the same.

The Aramaic word *hakana* and the Greek word *houto*, both translated as "so" in this verse, can mean: in this way, in this manner, thus—it answers the question "how," but not "how much." "For this is the manner in which God loved..."

There is no degree to God's love because it is infinite—*anything that can't be measured always looks the same*. It's indiscriminant—like the rays of the sun burning out in every possible direction and falling in exactly the same way on every person, place, and thing on the dayside of the planet. It can't be turned down, and it can't be turned off—like drinking from a fire hose, we get more than we could possibly ingest all at once; and like the air, it can't be avoided or outrun. All we can do is pretend it doesn't exist or that it doesn't apply and live as if that were true, continuing to use language that describes God's love in terms of degree and exclusivity.

God doesn't love the blind man any more, or you and me any less. God *can't* love us any more, and God *can't* love us any less than he does right now, at this moment, because his love is already and forever all it could ever be. There is nothing we can do to *make* God love us any more, and there's nothing we can do to make him love us any less: at our best moment, at our worst, God loves us exactly the same. God loves who we would call the most despicable person on the planet—the child rapist, the genocidal tyrant—as much as he loves us right now, and he's loved us at our worst moment, the moment whose memory still haunts our waking dreams, as much as who we'd call saints: Peter or Paul, Mother Teresa or Gandhi.

But even making the statement "God loves" is also deceptive because it masks a basic truth about God and his love.

God's love has to be always and forever the same, because *he* is always and forever the same; neither one can be anything other than what they are. For God, love is not a verb—it's a noun. Love isn't something God does; it's who he is. The very nature and identity of God is what we call love, what we experience as love. And any love we experience in life is God—part of that Source. As in 1 John 4:8, "The one who does not love does not know God, for God is love."

We *do* love: we can put it on or take off like a coat, but God *is* that thing called love; there is nothing to put on or take off that would change anything—he is love right down to the periodic table of the elements, to whatever passes for DNA or sub-atomic particles in God. This is why God's love can't be stopped, started, attenuated, amplified, altered, directed, or focused. It is our spiritual sun, a single source burning with abandon in every possible direction and with equal intensity and distribution. We can stand in its heat or we can seek shade, but love is unchanged by and unconcerned with such behavior—it continues to flood our world, waiting to warm us anytime we choose to come out of the shadows.

This fierce love is center stage in Yeshua's story of the prodigal son, the one who asks his father for his share of the inheritance so he can leave and live as he pleases, to seek his own identity elsewhere, outside the sameness of a dull, rural existence. It's hard for us modern Westerners to comprehend the impact of such a demand, but Yeshua's first listeners would have gasped at the arrogance of a son who was essentially saying that his own father was as good as dead to him, that he didn't care what happened to his family after he extracted the wealth that was intended to stay with the clan and support it. This was abomination to that community-based culture, an obscene insult—an unforgivable sin and a capital offense. Yet the father simply hands over his wealth, staring down the road long after his son is out of sight.

It's far too easy to keep our distance here, to think of this as just a colorful story about a first-century Jewish youth, but it's our story too, every single one of us. It's Jerry McGuire's story. We want our inheritance now, the wealth that comes from the leveling sameness of a perfect love, but we want our own personal power and imagined identity too. And in the process of trying to straddle that particular fence, we lose both. But like a phoenix rising from its ashes, it's in the moment of total loss that we find the seed of our salvation in the willingness to take an unthinkable risk.

When the prodigal son comes to this pass, reduced to living in a pigsty (the lowest, most unclean image a Jew could entertain) and eating the pigs' food scrounged from amid their excrement, he comes to his senses and decides to go back to his father—the one he said was as good as dead to him—and to his family—the one whose survival did not concern him. He understands the risk, the small odds of acceptance. He has seen *kezazah* performed, the ceremony in which the entire community breaks a clay pot in the path of a returning prodigal, ritually rejecting and blocking the way home. He decides not to even try to go back as a son, but only as a hired hand, intently rehearsing in his mind all the things he will say to try to convince his father to employ him.

But as soon as his father sees him crest the rise at the far edge of his land, we can imagine the strangled cry that escapes him as he dashes for the door and sprints the distance between them. We can see him gathering up his long robes, knobby white knees flashing as beard and shawl fly like banners in a stiff breeze.

Hebrew patriarchs didn't run; it was undignified. Hebrew patriarchs didn't expose their skin in public; it was indecent. Hebrew patriarchs didn't tolerate the unlawful disrespect of their children or a threat to their families, yet this father instantly looked decades younger as he closed the distance between him and his son at a dead run, throwing himself on the young man who must have braced for impact. The Scriptures, translated into English, merely tell us he "embraced him and kissed him." But what an embrace... what a kiss... The original words don't mean a single hug and kiss, but that he threw himself violently around his son's neck, that he couldn't stop kissing him, that a stinking young man stood stiffly in the middle of the road, blinking hard, as the venerable patriarch of his family, a ruling landowner, draped himself over him, becoming one with mud and excrement as he covered his hair, neck, and face with kisses and tears.

What to do? How to react when the walls of a tiny view of love come crashing down in a shower of tears and bearded kisses? Too good to be true: the son catches his breath and when he thinks he may have gained enough of his father's attention, carefully recites his monologue, the words rehearsed over and over as he made the journey home, the words we hear over and over ringing in our own ears: "I am no longer worthy to be called your son..." But even before his last word is fully pronounced, before he has time to worry over an answer, his father mercifully stops him, barking off orders and preparing a celebration as if he hadn't heard a single practiced word, saying with every action and nuance, "Relax, son. You're home. Everything's all right...you had me at hello."

This is our God. This is who he is.

Thank God. Any other God would not be Good News. Any other God would not describe the love that is the truth that makes us free.

But this love is also nothing to be trifled with; it's not for the faint of heart; it tolerates no compromise. It must be swallowed whole, all at once, or not at all. There is no way to bite off a piece, stick a toe in the water, or slowly turn up the heat. This love requires full extension, full commitment, complete abandon. It will take from us everything we think we are and give us everything God is in return. We can tell ourselves that this is a good trade, but we have to first be emptied before we can be filled. And from our side of the deal, before the trade is complete, before we've experienced what unity with God's identity really means, it just looks like death, the death of everything we've worked so hard to build and preserve—a deal-breaker for most of us.

The elder brother of the prodigal can't believe what he sees his father doing, is outraged at the allegiance his father is expressing to one so undeserving. It's not fair, it's not just—it's not fair to *him*, the one who tried so hard to earn and maintain his place in his father's house.

We can't believe it either.

Our behavior, our ability to keep a contract means nothing in the face of a love like this. This love is not fair. It is not just or even moral—it's just perfect. And when finally encountered, when we brace for its impact and feel its desperate embrace and hot kisses on our neck, how can we describe what we are beginning to understand? Brennan Manning, borrowing a phrase from G.K. Chesterton, calls it the "furious" love of God—a love that Chesterton wrote burned with such heat and passion that he couldn't distinguish it from the fires of hell itself.

As he prepared to enter the solitude of the monastery in the closing lines of his autobiography, *The Seven Storey Mountain*, Thomas Merton wrote:

> Everything that touches you shall burn you, and you will draw your hand away in pain, until you have withdrawn yourself from all things... Everything that can be desired will sear you, and brand you with a cautery, and you will fly from it in pain, to be alone. Every created joy will only come to you as pain, and you will die to all joy and be left alone. All the good things that other people love and desire and seek will come to you, but only as murderers to cut you off from the world and its preoccupations... That you may become the brother of God and learn to know the Christ of the burnt men.

The violence of these images may be shocking, but should not be surprising when laid against a love so complete, so utter, as to outrage us with its finality. And though Merton is not referring to God's love as much as the reality of monastic cloister, he is coming to grips with the life of seclusion he has chosen, the peeling away of all familiar half measures that stand between him and the undiluted experience of that love. Earning such a love, deserving such a love has no meaning when all the power of the universe couldn't contain or control the smallest part of its torrent. When we come face to face with such a love, there is no degree, no exclusion, no condition.

☽ ☾ ⊕ ⊕ ⊕

We've come a long way from "Jesus loves me, this I know..." and I realize many of you may be thinking that this goes too far, that these images in no way describe the love of the God with whom you're familiar.

And that's it exactly: they don't describe a familiar God.

The problem is not that we may be describing an unfamiliar God, but that *we're always describing God in terms of what is familiar.* The problem is not that we ever go too far, but that we can't ever go far enough, that there's no human way to go far enough in describing the allness of God's love. It can't be described; it can only be experienced, so we're left describing experiences and not the love itself. But the love exists as God exists, always in motion and unaffected by our experiences and always present and waiting for us to turn and embrace it. We get it all and all at once whenever we're ready to accept what it means to be beloved.

Henri Nouwen writes in *Life of the Beloved*, that the phrase...

'You are my Beloved' reveals the most intimate truth about all human beings, whether they belong to any particular tradition or not...all I want to say to you is 'You are the Beloved,' and all I hope is that you can hear these words as spoken to you with all the tenderness and force that love can hold. My only desire is to make these words reverberate in every corner of your being— 'You are the Beloved.'

We are all God's beloved; we are all God's favorite. We are all the center of God's universe, because no other position has any meaning. What would our lives be like if we could really trust our place with God, if we knew there was a love that we could always count on, the way we've always counted on our misery? A love that would never leave or forsake?

Even if we're still not sure we believe our belovedness, even if we're not sure we understand such a love at all, we can still act. We can drive a stake in the ground right here, right at the center of God's universe, right at the point of his perfect love. We can make a stand and resolve to let the world revolve around the reality of God's love and not the reverse, because the truth, the truth that will make us free, is that God's love is the only reality there is.

If we can begin to interpret everything we experience in life in terms of that love and not interpret that love in terms of all the brokenness we experience, we will begin to change. We will begin to do the things of which Yeshua spoke, but which we never dreamed possible—things that others will not believe or understand or even approve until our experience becomes theirs as well.

About five years ago, a friend of mine ended his marriage and not surprisingly, began his journey at the same time. The marriage had been failing for years, but more recently his wife had begun a relationship with another man that she was not willing to give up, and in her pain, had become more and more abusive to my friend and their children. As the sum of unhappiness in the family reached the breaking point, my friend realized he couldn't go on; found an apartment, wanted to move out quickly, and asked for my help. I was a newly ordained pastor at the time, and the irony of what I was being asked to do was not lost on me. But he was my friend so I rented a truck, and we packed it up, drove across town, unpacked it again.

I listened long to my friend pouring out his brokenness and anger. I remember him saying, "I just wish she were dead. I can picture her floating face down in the ocean. I wish she were dead." He saw her as the gravity, the center of all his and his family's pain, and he hated her for it. I could understand. I think we all could.

But fast-forward just three years. Right after my friend moved out, his ex-wife had moved her lover in with her and the children and now had a six-month-old son by him as well. And what was my friend's reaction? He was carrying a picture of that baby around in his wallet, he'd baby-sit for them whenever he was needed, he'd sometimes bring the boy to church with him and introduce him like a proud uncle. He would go to dinner with the whole family, celebrate birthdays and holidays together with them, and even began acting as a counselor at times between his ex-wife and her live-in companion. Today, nothing has changed as my friend sees himself and is accepted as part of an extended family with no real distinction between his children and theirs.

How do you get from wanting to see your estranged wife dead and floating face down in the ocean to babysitting the child of her lover and caring for him as if he were your own? In just a couple of years? I was there; I watched my friend's transformation, but I still can't tell you. He can't tell you either. Oh, he'll throw a lot of words at the subject in his fervor and enthusiasm, but he can't really explain it to anyone's satisfaction.

Most of his friends thought he was a doormat, completely duped or co-dependent. I've worried about him too, from time to time—that he's too attached, too present to relationships that really aren't his and can be taken away at any moment. But then, when doesn't this describe any and every relationship we can ever have in this life? What do we really control except our willingness to participate?

Somewhere along his journey, my friend encountered a love so real, so powerful and permanent that it burned away his pain, his need for fairness, his need to be "right" and justified in the eyes of others—replacing all that with the ability to take an unthinkable risk, to extend himself to someone who didn't deserve it any more than he did himself.

His friends still don't understand. They worry about him, alternating between shock and outrage, and at times think he's completely crazy. But my friend is the one walking around a few inches off the ground with a baby in his arms...

So who's crazy here?

☉ ☉ ⊕ ⊕ ⊕

An email arrived from a thirty-four-year-old Texas mother of three who was recently laid off from her full-time job and suffering a full-blown spiritual crisis:

> Some months I don't even allow myself to ponder the questions, because when I do, I cannot stop...in the bathroom crying out to God or whoever is in charge out there that may be listening. I have been in and out of depressions, unsure of anything. Searching for an elusive answer. But I've come to the realization that I may never find what I am looking for. I must say, and I hope you will not take offense, that I honestly don't even know if God exists...I am like a lost sheep at this time in my life. Crying out silently with questions that no man can answer. Who are we? Why are we here? Who am I? How can generations of people be lied to? My questions go even deeper and unfortunately I am told that it is a matter of faith to know the answers. The sad thing is that I want to have faith, but have none left. I am afraid of being deceived. Every single religious group out there thinks that they have the corner on the market of truth. But how can this be? In my heart, I want to go back to being nine years old and believing that there is a good God and there is a savior who cares for me even if no one else does... but I can't.

We corresponded for some weeks, and though she was always appreciative of my attempts, I never got the impression that I had explained anything to her satisfaction. I wanted so badly to cradle that little nine-year-old girl inside her and somehow let her know that everything was going to be all right, that answers can and do come in ways most unexpected. Maybe if I could just find the right words, I thought... After a while she just stopped writing.

Yeshua couldn't really explain it to anyone's satisfaction either, there are no words for such a job. In the throes of a pain so deep that "Who am I?" becomes a meaningless string of words, Yeshua's own words, "I and the Father are one," seem equally meaningless. It's only in the process of being loved, experiencing love, that an identification with that love and with the Source of that love begins to take on substance and meaning as the only possible answer to the question. *When I and this love are one* is a big moment, a moment when life makes sense.

In the face of everything I can't know, in the face of the uncertainty, pain, and panic, I can at least start with what I do know. I can at least do that. And if I listen carefully, if I read between the lines, Yeshua is always trying to tell me that no matter where I am in life, no matter what I'm feeling, no matter how much I think I've failed or how unworthy I am, how much I feel unlovely and therefore unlovable, how much I question whether God can really accept me or whether I can accept the risk of really laying myself down...at any time, at any moment, I can stop; I can turn around and re-present myself to God. Always. It's that simple and that difficult.

And in the moment I stop and turn to look, no matter how many times that may be, he will be right there or perhaps running up the road to tackle me. He'll be right there, because he always was and was never anywhere else. And he'll have a soft look on his face as I'm shifting and sweating and reeling off all the words I've rehearsed to try to explain myself, to try to convince him and persuade him to take me back—until the moment I'm ready to let him mercifully stop me and say close to my ear,

"Honey, relax...it's okay, it's all right. Hush now...

"You had me at hello."

CHALLENGE

God is love without degree or condition—unaffected by anything we do;
we can't make God love us more or less, we can only receive more or less.

TRADITION
God's love is expressed through his law;
obedience expresses our love in return.

Identity Gift

LAW

Love takes one's neighbor as one's other self...
Love demands a complete inner transformation, for without this we
cannot possibly come to identify ourselves with our brother.

Thomas Merton

All you need is...

WHAT? FILL IN THE BLANK HERE. THE BEATLES SAID LOVE. THE church says Jesus. But the New Testament says Jesus is God, and God is love, so if A equals B and B equals C—are we back to love?

When the church says we need Jesus, it traditionally means we need the blood of Jesus, the acceptance of the substitution of his death for ours, the acknowledgement of his Godhood, all of which is the prerequisite to salvation, the avoidance of an eternity in hell. And when Yeshua said he was the Way, the truth, and the life, and no one comes to the Father but through him, what he meant by that has been endlessly debated, but theologically, we conflate the two concepts cementing the connection between a creedal Jesus, atoning sacrifice, and salvation/heaven.

It's a contract of sorts. The New Testament contains the text of the contract, the obligations and benefits of both parties—God and us; if we agree to the terms of the contract and sign the bottom line, God will perform his obligations as long as we perform ours and don't breach the contract.

We have become "Contractual Christians."

We can call ourselves Christian and expect heaven as reward if we have signed the contract, agreed to belief in the "essentials" of the faith from virgin birth to bodily resurrection, and live our lives according to the terms therein. It's as if we can legally bind God, make him accountable, make him predictable, make him owe us his favor if we believe just right, pray just right, live just right...

Now, you may protest: of course that's not what I believe, because the Scriptures also say that salvation is a free gift. Or as Paul states it in Ephesians, it's by grace, God's unconditional love that we are saved, not by works so none of us can boast about our achievements. But think again. Is our acceptance of God's gift, out of which flows a life that looks like Christ, really enough in our theology to secure the heaven of God's acceptance of us without the signing of the contract as well?

When I strayed from Catholicism, I remember my mother telling me "being good is not enough;" I needed to remain covered under the sacraments of the "one true church." Mormons and Jehovah's Witnesses believe they are following Jesus, but mainstream Christians believe they are still "unsaved," unacceptable to God, because they are following the "wrong" Jesus, one who does not conform to orthodox theological standards and therefore has "no power to save." Looked at this way, our theological concepts, ideas we hold in our minds are ultimately what make us acceptable to God. Or as Marcus Borg has written, it's "salvation by syllables."

God's love may have given us the contract, but mere love is not enough to fulfill it because we're all born sinners and the scales of God's justice must first be balanced before love can have its way. And though justice is certainly the highest good in a macro sense, with groups of people, we forget that it is a wholly inadequate expression of love in the micro, in one-on-one relationships. Yeshua took great pains to show us that he and his Father don't love each of us individually with mere justice but with mercy and compassion, and even though he repeatedly asked us all to do the same with each other, we can't seem to shake our legalistic tendencies, living as if our faith could be contained in a bulleted list.

With this logic, God is bound by, even slave to, the legal edge of his own justice—he is not free to exercise mercy and compassion as he may wish with any one individual. Traditional Christian theology teaches that this is exactly the purpose of the crucifixion: the ultimate blood sacrifice that balanced the legal scales for those who believe—and so we come back to the contract, a contract written in blood. And though I use some hyperbole to make the point, the point remains.

It seems what we as a church give with one hand, we take away with the other, like a schizophrenic, split personality or bi-polar condition that constantly shifts us back and forth between faith and works and love and obligation. God's love and ultimate acceptance is free, but only "works" for us if we agree to believe a certain way and live a certain way.

I received an email from a twenty-something man working in ministry for years both in churches and "freelance" parachurch programs he founded in his community. Seeing himself as part of the "progressive" church, those Christians seriously questioning existing church doctrine and practice, he is planning to launch a church of his own. As a first step, he says he feels the need to write a statement of faith, since one of the main criticisms of the progressive church is its lack of stated doctrine—and he's absolutely right.

But the criticism of progressive churches by those in more orthodox circles for not defining concrete doctrines is not on point: what *should* be criticized is that progressive leaders have not clearly stated *why* they have not relied on concrete doctrinal statements. Emphasizing an intellectual statement of faith, feeling the *need* for a statement of faith as a standard for inclusion is a further sign that we have left the original intent of Jewish teaching, of Yeshua's teaching, of James' teaching: that faith is *lived out* and not merely thought out. That a person of faith is defined more clearly by relational choices than by mental assent.

It's the contractual and legal attitude we have developed playing itself out once again: as if these articles of faith we place on paper have some sort of saving properties without which God won't accept us; as if Yeshua's Way were simply a theological litmus test for salvation and not what he demonstrated—a quality of life lived in God's presence. When pressed for a statement of faith in Matthew 22, for the essentials, the "greatest commandment," all Yeshua stated was to love God with everything available and each other as ourselves—anything else was commentary.

The truth about statements of faith is that they do much more to divide and separate people of faith than they ever do to unite believers—pointing us toward abstract concepts rather than concrete moments with each other. Maybe we can take a cue from the Eastern Orthodox Churches where theology and doctrine function and exist to exclude outright error that would immediately harm people's lives, and not to advance essential beliefs that God would use to exclude *us*. From that Eastern perspective, we are not saved by the thoughts in our heads, but by living more and more closely mirrored in God's presence, which is experienced as the quality of life that Yeshua calls *Kingdom*.

☽ ☾ ⊕ ⊕ ⊕

At a recent church service I attended, the associate pastor prayed between songs during worship and then said, "If you could know how much God loves you for just a moment, you'd be laid out on the floor. I pray that God will show all of us the extent of his beautiful love." Just one song later, in the next lull, he again prayed and said, "When Yeshua comes back, he won't come peaceably. He'll have a sword in his mouth. He's going to slay the wicked. You're going to want to be on the right side."

That he could juxtapose these two messages in the space of just one song; that he saw no contradiction, no dissonance in them; that no one in the church reacted or seemed fazed at all by his words, indicates just how deep the schizophrenia goes.

It's enough to paint any of us into theological corners from which assurance of God's mercy and compassion seems forever out of reach. If we say we believe, but don't always live according to the contract, then it's possible we never believed in the first place, nullifying the contract. Or if we aren't living in accordance with the contract beforehand, is it possible to sign in good faith until we do? A pastor and friend of mine used to say, "Don't clean your fish before you catch them." I could paraphrase him by saying: don't keep trying to win the favor of a God who is already and forever yours. But we do, repeatedly, don't we?

Then on the other hand, we say: the good life of the believer is not a prerequisite to God's love, but will flow out of that love, the love now actualized in the life of the saved believer. But then where does that same life of love come from in those who have the love but not the contract? Those of other denominations or other religions? Are they "saved" too? And so we come back to the contract once more.

Such arguments have flourished all through the history of the church. Martin Luther ranted against the book of James saying its focus on human works came at the expense of faith. In the theology of Augustine, we should love God and do as we please, but Pelagius, appalled at the licentious behavior of Roman Christians, focused so heavily on good works that he was accused of teaching that grace was no more than humans freely choosing to follow law. Predestination and "once saved always saved" perseverance of the saints defined Calvin's adherents against the opposing free will emphasis of Arminius. These arguments were serious because they defined the terms of the contract, but they still haven't been resolved and won't be resolved here or ever—because they can't be.

"If God is all-powerful, can he make a rock so heavy he can't lift it?" When we try to resolve a question like this, we are caught in a logical bind. Like one of those Chinese finger traps we loved as children—they only gripped tighter the more we pulled. But stop pulling, and instantly we break the tension by moving in the opposite direction of our apparent escape.

Whenever we come to a logical paradox, a mental trap from which there is no intellectual escape, such as the debate between faith and works or predestination and free will, it's because we've missed a turn somewhere long before we got to the impasse. We've used a faulty assumption or a logical premise where logic is no longer relevant. Common sense must step in and say that our very *method* of engaging the paradox is faulty and will never reflect the reality of life in God's presence. The more we let Yeshua speak from his Hebrew roots, the more we realize that our faith is not a logical certainty, can't be won in an either-or debate, only experienced in a both-and embrace. And only as we push in the opposite direction of our apparent escape do we find the freedom Yeshua promises.

Having lost the connection to our Eastern, Jewish roots by the mid-second century—after the two Jewish-Roman wars that destroyed the temple, Jerusalem, the entire nation of Israel, and the traditional Jewish way of life—gentile Christianity was already hopelessly trying to make sense of Yeshua's Eastern teaching through a Western mindset. This age-old misunderstanding has ironically re-established the legal view of God that Yeshua worked so hard to deconstruct as he battled the Pharisaic tradition and has had one main and disastrous effect: *it has diminished our understand-*

ing of God's love. How can we experience a love that is unconditional, when the implied contract stipulates conditions that only bind us tighter the harder we pull?

It all comes down to this: knowing the truth of God's love.

Whatever side of these theological fences we choose to place ourselves, if what we have chosen to believe about God's nature allows us to accept and live life on its own terms with a baseline contentment experienced as the trust that all will be ultimately well, nothing more needs saying. If it's not broke, don't fix it. But ideas do have consequences, and the fact is, for many people with whom I've worked, a contractual view of our relationship with God has been devastating. How do we truly trust a love we say is free, but for which we must also contract to receive? Though the thoughts in our head don't "save" us, they certainly do determine our perception of reality. Experiencing the truth of God's love lifts it out of the confines of the contract and lets it expand to full size. Anything short of that fullness keeps us living in fear, the suburbs of hell.

First person experience, not acceptance of second or third person teaching is the key; there is no substitute—it's the whole point of the spiritual journey. And it's exactly what Yeshua is saying from a Hebrew context when he says that he is the way, truth, and light, and no one comes to the Father but through *him*—through the way to truth and light he embodies. Ancient Jews viewed life as function over form. How people and things functioned defined them, not physical attributes. Yeshua's first followers told us how deeply they understood Yeshua's function by calling themselves not Christians or even followers of Yeshua, but "Followers of the *Way*," *talmidey orha*, followers of the only Way home to their Father.

A name, *shem*, to an ancient Jew was deeply significant: it revealed the inner, defining essence of a person or place. We need to fully absorb the significance of the name those who walked with Yeshua gave themselves, or we will misunderstand Yeshua's words at

John 14. If we believe that "Jesus as only way" points to his form, theological attributes, rather than his function, a way of living life that leads to truth and light, we'll miss the essence of Kingdom, the quality of life always available right herenow in the direct experience of God's presence, which can never be separated from his love.

It's not that traditional Western Christian theology is wrong. It's that it is only right if it points toward and supports an active *experience* of God's love and presence, if it *never takes the place* of such an experience of God's love and presence, if it *never presents or implies a false view* of God's love and presence.

> Any theology can only point toward God's love;
> it doesn't guarantee it.

How could it? How is it possible to contract for something that is already freely abundant? Would we sign a contract granting us access, for a fee, to air and sunshine? Until those commodities were somehow restricted, such a contract would be meaningless.

Is there is a contract with God?

If all the religious words you've ever read have brought you to the point of asking this one question, then they have value—but only if. Because as long as the contract remains, how is God's love freely offered? If we believe there's a contract, don't we also believe if we've earned our righteousness, we are entitled, and if we haven't, we are victims of our own guilt? If we're entitled, there is no gratitude; if we're victims, there is no growth. Law is like that: binary, dualistic, either-or... But Yeshua's Kingdom *embraces* gratitude and growth, is *made of* gratitude and growth along its Way of partnership and oneness with God.

Partnership. Can we really presume to partner with God?

The Aramaic word Yeshua chose to describe Kingdom: *malkutha*, refers not to place or territory, but the principles by which the king reigns. It is an expression of the quality of the reign of a monarch who serves his people in a two-way flow of shared purpose and was used to describe the God-centered reigns of Israel's righteous kings. This word stands in contrast to *mamlacha*, another Hebrew word for kingdom that refers to a one-way, dictatorial, possibly abusive reign and used to describe the rule of non-God centered or gentile kings.

By choosing *malkutha*, Yeshua portrays a quality of life that is possible for people who share his Father's principles and function as one with him right herenow. Until we understand the immediacy and partnership in Yeshua's definition of Kingdom—that it's not a place in a future setting but an always available state of being—we'll never understand how we are loved, because as long as we're waiting for it to be granted, we're not experiencing the flow of shared purpose and being that is the Father's love.

How *do* we receive love?

How do I give you the ability to play guitar, to dance, to speak a second language? Such things are not bestowed, but learned through experience. How can I give you love? Love is not given directly; the effects of love's choices are experienced, and either beloved begins to identify with lover or not.

We can almost hear Yeshua saying, I can lead you and your horse to water, but I can't make either of you drink. I can throw the key to your prison cell inside the bars, but I can't make you use it. I can even open the door of your cell, physically pull you out and drop you off on a street corner downtown, but I can't make you free. I can give you all I have to give, save you from certain death, but I can't make you grateful. I can tell you you're forgiven and pardon you, commute your sentence, but I can't assuage the guilt you feel or make you comfortable in any of your relationships again. I can love you with all that is in me, but I can't make you love me or anyone else in return. I can't do any of these things any more than I can make a suckling infant walk and talk before muscle and synapse are ready...

...and God can't either.

Because to do so would change the definition of love itself—of who and what God is *him*self. Love is not the one-way, dictatorial rule of *mamlacha*. If it's dictated or coerced in any way, it's no longer love. Love, forgiveness, liberation, and salvation are the volitional reflection of those kingly qualities in us, in the two-way relationship and partnership of *malkutha*, or they are nothing at all. The potential exists in us; God put it there. And he's always aware of those seeds of potential ripeness no matter how green or rotten we outwardly appear to all concerned.

A contract with God is meaningless, because all God is and has is not for sale; it can't be restricted; it can't be bestowed; it can only be realized when the student is ready and decides to make his or her desire and purpose the same as God's. This is the truth that will make us free. And it is also the truth that a legal contract obscures with its promise of guaranteed results in exchange for fees or in-kind trade. God and love have no meaning or existence in such an environment.

☉ ⏀ ⊕ ⊕ ⊘

When we read the word *disciple* or *follower* in our New Testament versions, the Aramaic word behind the Greek behind the English is *talmid* or *talmidim* in the plural. There really is no concept in contemporary Western life that is comparable to *talmid*. We translate this word as disciple or follower, but there is no place in our culture for someone who voluntarily seeks to so fully submit and identify with a master in all areas of life as to drop everything and completely dedicate his or her life to becoming like the master in every way—as did Yeshua's first *talmidim* who dropped their nets and followed at his word.

Cloistered monastics could qualify as *talmidim* for the most part, but they are now quite foreign to contemporary Western culture. There is the also-rare example of a trade apprentice who spends years with the master craftsman learning every aspect of the craft, and there is the recruit at boot camp whose own identity (along with clothes, hair, and anything else that is personal and individual) is stripped away to be replaced by that of the soldier. But even these fall short. Religious cults are defined by the practice of separating their subjects from everything in their former lives and forcing an identity change on them, but this is not usually a volitional, conscious process on the part of the follower, and if it's coerced or manipulated, it produces mindless followers, not *talmidim*.

In the last two verses of Matthew, when Yeshua tells us to go make disciples—*talmidim*—of people throughout the world, he is calling us to first become *talmidim* ourselves, to dedicate ourselves to the task of living, eating, sleeping, working, playing, loving, suffering, bleeding, and breathing every moment of our lives with God so that his deepest purpose becomes ours, or better, that we *become* his purpose, his *sebyana*—his will.

Once again, Yeshua's Aramaic word choice guides us. The Aramaic word *sebyana* is typically translated "will," but rather than being a legal term or an authoritarian mandate, was understood as pleasure, delight, desire, and deepest purpose—that which defines essential qualities, identity. Only when what we desire most, what we can't imagine doing without, what animates us and gives us the most pleasure and sense of purpose is exactly what animates God, can we encourage and show others, all others, how to do the same. We can only offer what we already possess, and only a true *talmid* can offer the experience of the *talmidim*.

When we read the Great Commission passage through Western eyes, we can make the mistake of thinking that the "evangelism" Yeshua is commanding is limited to simply converting people to a certain system of belief, or a pledge of allegiance to a certain creed with the power to "save." We sincerely believe we can count the number of people saved by counting the number of people who recite a conversion prayer during a weekend rally. But through Aramaic eyes, Yeshua's gospel is not a creed at all; it's not a proposition or a statement of faith. It's a dynamic call to a Way of life. Yeshua's self-described life as the *talmid* of his Father in heaven is at once the way and the truth and the life for us all. No one can come to the Father but through Yeshua, through his Way of living in the practice of the presence of God.

This living in Kingdom—the awareness of *Emmanuel*, of "God-with-us," this *talmid*, this person of the Way, is so fully identified with the Father as to be functionally one with him. Like thinking in a second language, where thoughts and sentences are automatically and correctly formed without having to translate first mentally, the true *talmid*, the true disciple, does not have to think about how Law or ethics "translate" into correct choices. Such choices are automatic response because the deepest purpose and pleasure of the *talmid* has become the same as God's.

Your kingdom come, your will be done as in heaven, so on earth is Yeshua's petition for the *oneing*, confluence of wills between heaven and earth, fully realized when he says that when you've seen me, you've seen the Father. Seeing Yeshua is functionally the same as seeing the Father, because we will never get an answer or choice or action from Yeshua that we wouldn't get from the Father himself.

But even after years of walking with Yeshua as his *talmidim*, his closest companions still didn't understand. At John 14, Philip asks Yeshua to "show us the Father" and that "will be enough for us." In one of the most human moments in the New Testament, Yeshua's frustration shows right through the understated text. You can almost see him slapping his forehead as his voice rises in pitch and volume: "Have I been so long with you, and yet you have not come to know me, Philip? He who has seen me has seen the Father; how can you say, 'Show us the Father?'"

As long as Philip had traveled with Yeshua, lived with him night and day, ate with him, laughed with him, listened to him, loved him, he was not yet *talmid*. He still didn't understand Yeshua's intent, that Yeshua and the Father were one, that Yeshua shared his Father's *sebyana*. That he, Philip, and we, all of us, could do the same and become one with Yeshua and the Father, doing the same things we see Yeshua doing—and greater things even than those as he tells us just three verses later. Though different in form, by becoming indistinguishable in intent and action, identification with God is not beyond our grasp.

"Being good is not enough," is meant to set our belief in the contract. But the assumption here is deceiving. The New Testament tells us that it's not by creed or works at all that we are "saved," and the salvation written into Scripture from a Hebrew mindset means spiritual liberation that is never relegated to a future life or separated from the quality of our lives herenow. Being "good" *is* enough, if we are simply living our moments in conscious identification with God.

Augustine again: *love God and do as you please*, because once you have responded to the unconditional flow of God's love, have become identified with that love, doing what you please will always look like Yeshua, will look like law and contract without the need for either.

Obedience to law is what is not enough...and the subconscious security of an implied contract with God, however comforting at first, locks us in a legal mindset that only grips us tighter in the fear of possible punishment the harder we pull to break free.

Only when we push in the opposite direction of our apparent escape, graduate from obedience-to-law to identification-with-Lawgiver, do we find ourselves at Yeshua's trailhead.

The salvation Yeshua is speaking of—as all Hebrews understood—is the spiritual liberation, the freedom from fear that allows us to throw ourselves into life and relationship with complete abandon. James called it the *law of liberty* (James 1:25), a contradiction in terms that speaks of a quality of following that never feels like restriction or limitation, but simply the enactment of anything and everything you ever wanted to do and be.

It's much more than our two-dimensional concept of a mere salvation from hell's punishment, and Yeshua's first *talmidim*, the followers of the Way, knew that salvation is not the reward for a correct mental belief, but a Way of living that begins with a mental belief that leads to the action of faith that leads to the experience of trust: the displacement of our fear that allows us to see who God really is, and ourselves in him.

It's not identity *theft*, but identity *gift*. We give our identity to God, and he gives his to us.

A very good trade.

CHALLENGE

Law applies only until we graduate from conformance to transformance: making obedience obsolete by fully identifying with the Lawgiver.

TRADITION
We know God's intent through creed and doctrine;
on our own, we risk being led into error.

Convictions of the Heart

ENGAGEMENT

Go become convinced of what you're convinced of.

Emery Tang

AT ONE OF THE MOST DIFFICULT AND CRITICAL POINTS IN MY LIFE, I found a retreat center run by the Franciscans that still occupies a hill at the back of a canyon emptying out onto the coast at Malibu. At a time when my world and life were literally dissolving before my eyes, I remembered the white cross that I'd seen so many times, seemingly suspended mid-air against the backdrop of the mountains—a fleeting image barely entered into consciousness as my car sped along Coast Highway on the way to somewhere else. Now that cross was calling me, and one day I just drove, keeping it in the center of my windshield until the road stopped at Serra Retreat. It became for me all that word implied: a haven, a rest, a redoubt, even a fortress for a time.

Sometimes I would just show up, book a room, and stay for a few days. Sometimes I would join a group in their scheduled retreat for a weekend; sometimes I would participate and sometimes just lurk and listen. But always, I would engage in the silence and the peace, in the early morning masses often with only three or four of us present...and always before bed I would run down the hill and through the dark, silent streets of the canyon—looking over my shoulder through warmly lit windows and wondering what sort of people could afford such homes, and through the black canopy of trees to the stars beyond and wondering what sort of God could afford me.

And always, there were the friars, the Franciscan priests and brothers who ran the center and directed the retreats. They moved about the red-tiled Spanish buildings in their brown, hooded robes to a beat that seemed to make time stand still and led further into the otherworldliness of the place.

The director of the retreat center was a first generation Chinese-American, who had been a Franciscan priest for almost fifty years and leading the retreat center for the last ten of those. Chinese had been his first language, and he was still fluent, both in the language and all the traditions his parents had brought with them across the Pacific. He was an artist: his Chinese calligraphy was stunning and was printed along with his photography and writings in several books on sale in the gift shop off the main lobby. In every way, from his art to his thinking and spirituality to the subtly Chinese inflection and cadence of his English, he was a man who stood directly astride East and West in a way I had never encountered.

He had skin just a few shades lighter than his robe and a completely shaven head, immense hands that seemed to cover his entire scalp as he often did, as if holding his head in place while thinking between sentences. His ears bent slightly outward at the tips so that in his dark brown robe with the hood draped down his back and stark white rope tied around his waist, he looked for all the world like a six-foot Yoda. Everything about him seemed to fit together into a cohesive whole, to move step by step in a single direction—a direction that intrigued me, but which I was not yet prepared to follow. Even his name, Emery Tang, provided the initials ET that he had mounted in wooden letters on his office door.

ET was always getting into trouble. ET didn't think as regular Catholics thought or teach as regular Catholics taught. He had some pretty unorthodox ideas about theology and life that he wasn't in the least bit shy about sharing, which in turn caused a fairly regular stream of letters to arrive at the chancery office alternately complaining about him and demanding his removal. I was amazed he seemed to see no contradiction in being a Catholic priest and having such un-Catholic ideas.

I asked him why he remained but he just laughed and said he'd been a priest for nearly fifty years and would die a priest. He loved being a priest and loved his church even as he mourned for the state of many of its people. Not only did he believe there was no reason to leave the church and his vocation because of his convictions, he believed the only chance for the revitalization of the church was from the inside out—that he needed to remain inside, a seed, a catalyst for change. He told me that he was trying with everything in him to be released from his duty at the retreat center so he would be free to work with younger people who didn't regularly attend retreats, but still had open minds and hearts and ears to hear. He said he had another ten good years left, and he wanted to really make them count. I remember being very glad he was right where I could find him, but also silently celebrated with him a few years later when he was finally released.

Though he never expressed it as such, ET was always getting into trouble because in word, action, and thought, he wouldn't abide anything that restricted or contradicted a view of love so vast that it would be years before I started to see. But there was no insistence from him that I see what he saw at all. Just a gentle but steady pull from the choice of his words and quality of his presence, a phrasing and posture just alien enough to keep bringing glimpses of something that wouldn't quite resolve, remaining securely in periphery.

Maybe it was easier for him to reject the hyper intellectual and legal tone of Western thought and practice because there was so still much East in him from birth. Or because he was such a creative artist. Or maybe his fifty years swimming around in that brown robe had led him to places where love that big couldn't hide. Or all the above.

But one Saturday, while leading discussion among a group of about fifty middle-aged to elderly men who booked the same weekend from the same diocese every year for as long as anyone's memory held, ET asked a big question to anyone and everyone in the room. "Why did Jesus come?" he wanted to know. Silence for a few beats then some hands went up.

"To die for our sins," came the response right out of the Baltimore Catechism.

It was one of those Yeshua and Philip moments where the frustration of all the years spent uncomprehendingly together breaks through to the surface of things. With hands already covering his head, ET said, "No, no, no, no... Jesus didn't come to die for our sins—what kind of Father sends his son only to die? Jesus came to show us perfect love." And trying to develop his thoughts over their objections, as murmurs grew into angry retorts, ET finally asked another big question: why they bothered coming to retreat year after year, to the same place time after time, thinking the same thoughts and never growing—that next year they should just stay home. I'm sure the chancery mailbag was quite full over the following week.

It was one of my weekends for lurking and listening, but I intently followed the exchange. In all my catechism and Bible study over thirty plus years, I'd never been asked or stopped to consider God's intent—what he intended for us, for Yeshua—the intent behind Yeshua's life and mission. And though I, as student, was not ready at that moment to grasp ET's words, he knew just what to tell me later, alone in his office, when he held up his big hand to my objections and simply said:

"All I can tell you is what I've become convinced of. Go become convinced of what you're convinced of."

Some things in life are not transferable, but at least the mess my life had become had created in me the burning need to be convinced of *some*thing. To be able to state that thing, whatever it was, with the conviction of ET suddenly felt like life itself. There was no turning back as I set out to become convinced of what I was convinced of.

And as I now teach and write and work, I am acutely aware of my own limitations, the limitations of anyone who tries to communicate an idea to another human. The things I am now convinced of can be spoken and written down, but not bestowed. Nor should they be. Matters can be brought to our attention, we can even decide to believe them, but we'll never speak them with ET's conviction or Yeshua's authority, and we'll never displace the fear in our lives until we've traveled the journey ourselves, tasted and seen for ourselves the goodness of God's love.

Encouraging engagement in the journey is the teacher's gift, not the imparting of information.

⊙ ⊙ ⊕ ⊕ ⊕

In emphasizing personal conviction, it may seem I am minimizing the importance of the church and religion, but really it's an attempt to pull the pendulum back to center. Though church and religion were never meant to be an end in themselves, they can provide the community and structure we all need to experience the discipline, accountability, and service that bring us face to face with our own identity, meaning, and purpose. But our churches become unhealthy to the degree they allow the people within them to remain fearful and passive, and they become irrelevant to the degree they minimize Yeshua's critical emphasis on becoming intimately engaged in the personal experience of God's love.

As Western churches have shifted into an increasing emphasis on an intellectual understanding of doctrine and scripture and the managing of people's unlawful behavior, people have essentially been taught that their faith is about mental acceptance of a theological idea and their behavior is about obedience to law, like a contract with God. In such a mental and legal environment, people aren't encouraged to engage and experience the transformational freedom that Yeshua is constantly saying is available right herenow.

If we haven't been exposed to the full scope of Christian thought, we tend to think that the culture and worldview of our own church is all there is. But in another instance of the great divide between East and West, this time within Christianity itself, Eastern Orthodoxy and Assyrian churches—Aramaic speaking churches established in the first century among the descendants of Assyria in what is now northern Syria, Iraq, and Iran—have a very different outlook on spirituality than Western Catholic and Protestant counterparts. Where we in the West tend to see sin, grace, and salvation ultimately in legal terms as a balancing of God's justice, Eastern churches understand them as part of a larger process of spiritual recovery—a lifelong restoration of unity with God that was lost through the separation that is sin.

Eastern churches recall Yeshua teaching a truth that had to be experienced personally in a one-on-one relationship with God, not grasped intellectually through precise theological definitions. They do hold theological beliefs, of course. But in the West, where written theology is understood as accurate portrayals of God's nature and often used as a litmus test, the criteria for judging a person's acceptability to both church and God, in the East, theology is primarily used to exclude outright error that harms lives and relationships. God can't be contained in an idea, so theology is about narrowing the playing field, placing guardrails at the shoulders of the road before setting off to become convinced of what we're convinced of. Far from being passive or vicarious, the Eastern concept of salvation culminates experientially in *theosis*, a Greek word that can be translated as *deification*. Not that people become God, but that they become one with God's life and purpose.

This worldview can sound a bit abstract or esoteric, but the effects that flow from it are certainly not. The difference between adhering to creed and contract and actively pursuing oneness with the Father's love and Spirit herenow is profound. It's the difference between experiencing Yeshua's truth in the first person or not, of being made free or not. It's the difference between white-knuckled abstinence and full recovery. The Eastern Church hears Yeshua saying that our salvation won't be found in written theology, our abstract conceptions of God, but in the give and take of a living relationship and is calling us to go back to the future with them.

A local Evangelical pastor recently converted to Eastern Orthodoxy prompting many to leave his church, but others, especially young people, have been gravitating toward and have become actively involved in the activities and events this church and others are sponsoring that are specifically designed to further the process of *theosis*, what we might call spiritual recovery—a process that the West has largely ignored. Until recently, Orthodox church growth in the United States was mainly fueled by immigration and marriage, but now up to a third of all US Orthodox priests are converts, close to half of seminary students are converts, and a third of the parishes of one Orthodox denomination were founded after 1990 with a large portion of membership under the age of forty. Many of these converts speak of the beauty of the liturgy and a theology that gives shelter from the doctrinal battles raging in other denominations. And though these numbers may still be relatively small, they point to a growing hunger for and a dawning realization of much more to our faith than creed and contract.

The role church plays in society and in our lives should not be minimized, but it seems our spiritual practices desperately need to be revitalized, giving people permission and empowerment to engage their own journeys to conviction. I've often heard that "sitting in church can no more make you a Christian than sitting in your garage will make you a car." And yet we often live as if that were true. In a passive approach to spirituality, we believe sitting in the security of creed and contract makes us saved and acceptable to God. And it's our Western understanding of the details of Scripture that has made this possible.

This is why ET's question was so incisive and so hard to answer: "Why did Jesus come?" If we can know God's original intent, we can find his purpose; if we know his purpose, we can better interpret the Scriptures and better formulate a theology that points in the same direction. But knowing God's intent? Intellectually, it sounds like presumption bordering on blasphemy, but if we have ears to hear, Yeshua is showing us another way of knowing.

Just before his arrest and execution, Yeshua prays one last great prayer at John 17. With the focus of a man nearing the end of his life, he prays:

I do not ask for these only, but also for those who will believe in me through their word, that they may all be one, just as you, Father, are in me, and I in you, that they also may be in us, so that the world may believe that you have sent me. The glory that you have given me I have given to them, that they may be one even as we are one, I in them and you in me, that they may become perfectly one, so that the world may know that you sent me and loved them even as you loved me... (ESV)

Yeshua prays for a unity that is only available to those willing to become *talmidim*, Aramaic for followers willing to deeply engage his purpose as a new way of life. And he is saying as straightforwardly as anywhere in Scripture that this unity *is* his purpose and mission. Unity is why he came, because to demonstrate the unity of God is to demonstrate the perfect love of God: "...so that the world may know that you sent me, and loved them, even as you have loved me." If Yeshua came to show us perfect love—perfect unity—then following his Way is living each day as if that love-unity is already our purpose as well. When our purpose has become the same as God's purpose, the intent of each choice we make becomes clear in a way we could never intellectually presume.

This unity does not present as a formal agreement or contract. How could it? The strength of any legal agreement always lies in the power to punish, and any relationship with God based in fear of punishment is "not perfected in love," 1 John 4, and can only offer obedience, never the fearless vulnerability of the unity of John 17.

How would our understanding of the most fundamental Christian precepts change as we move from law to love? The death of Yeshua on the cross with the intent of showing perfect love can be seen in greatest fullness as the inevitable result of that love, the ultimate vulnerability of a life that holds nothing back from the beloved, that holds no value in self that is not reflected in other: "Greater love has no one than this, that one lay down his life for his friends." If God *is* love as 1 John 4 tells us, then God's intent and purpose couldn't be anything else, and if Yeshua is one with the Father, as instrument of God's intent, Yeshua's purpose moves beyond death to life, love, and the preservation of both.

Looking through love's intent, Yeshua didn't come to die; he came to live—and his death, as the prerequisite to rebirth into new life, was also part of his Way of showing us how to live in perfect love, unity, and the endless promise of resurrection. When viewed from outside the contract, Yeshua's sacrifice brings us emphatically into the presence of a life lived with the absolute transparency and vulnerability that removes anything standing in the way of unity, of a love that has no limits and no cessation—a love that can't be bought or bartered because it is always and forever free.

In other words, regardless of how they are theologically expressed, Yeshua's death and sacrifice are fully understood when they point toward and support an active experience of God's love and presence; when they never take the place of such an experience of God's love and presence; and when they never present or imply a false view of God's love and presence.

> It's our entrance into Kingdom with which
> Yeshua and the Father are concerned,
> not our understanding of how we arrived.

These are things of which I've become convinced. I can't prove them; I can only tell you. It is up to each of us to go become convinced of what we are convinced of. But we need to be ruthlessly honest with ourselves as we proceed. Have we cut all the way to the bone in our search for the truth of God's intent and purpose? Have we allowed that intent and purpose to become the deepest convictions of our hearts?

How do we know when what we're convinced of has moved from beliefs in the head to convictions of the heart?

When we can stop compulsively looking for intellectual proof that by definition could never contain or convey our experience; when we can stop trying to *persuade others* of our beliefs, allow them the grace of their own journeys; when we find ourselves at the smile point, the place where love is no longer hard work but outright play and fear is no longer ruling our choices and attitudes; when we are living the gospel for all to see, not just believing it as a concept—preaching that gospel continuously but only using words where necessary, as the founder of ET's Franciscan order pleaded; when we can begin to trust and enjoy the ride... These are our benchmarks, clues to knowing whether our convictions, the truth we've come to know, is truth with the power to make us free.

⊙ ⊕ ⊕ ⊕ ⊕

This life we have been given is the greatest thrill ride ever devised. We haven't been given the choice to ride or not—if we're breathing, we're riding. But we do have the choice to enjoy or not. And like any theme park ride, we can only enjoy it to the extent we believe we'll survive it.

A good ride must be scary enough to whiten our knuckles and widen our eyes, but not so scary that we ever stop believing we'll see our parents smiling and waving as the car comes to a complete stop. We trust engineers and builders to use designs and materials that will support us; we trust government agencies to oversee and guarantee our safety or we'd never have chosen to ride in the first place. If for one second we thought something was wrong, if we were to see a missing section of track or a loose bolt, thrill becomes terror as we grip the safety bar and make silent bargains with God to bring us through.

The ride of our lives is no different. How can we live and love with abandon while fearing that our Father won't be there smiling and waving, as our ride comes to a stop with that last jolt? The fact that we find it easier to trust human engineers than the Engineer of the universe speaks volumes about our view of God and the quality of his love.

It seems we have trust issues with God. We doubt our ability to live up to the impossible standards of his justice, and we doubt his ability to live up to the impossible standards of his love—to tear up our implied contracts and simply open his arms.

Our mistrust limits us and our relationships in ways impossible to see from inside a contract that binds or outside a conviction that liberates. How can we know if the convictions of our hearts are the same as God's? We can begin by asking ourselves one simple question... *Are we enjoying the ride?*

That will tell us all we need to know.

CHALLENGE
Creed and doctrine are only launch pad and guardrail;
engagement with the unity at the heart of life convinces us of truth.

TRADITION
The teachings of Scripture are timeless;
they apply literally to every situation anywhere, anywhen.

Message in a Bottle

INTERPRETATION

The message is in the bottle; it's not the bottle itself.

IT OFTEN SEEMS THAT THE MOST IMPORTANT THINGS, THE MOST fundamental things in life come in pairs. In the ancient symbolism of numbers, two means generation or production, and so that which produces and preserves life, comes from pairs of things. Scripture tells of Adam and Eve, the original pair of humans, generating life for the billions of us who follow; Noah bringing pairs of every living thing into the ark to preserve that life; Yeshua in Luke 10 sending out seventy of his *talmidim* two by two ahead of himself to prepare the way for rebirth into new life.

It even seems that the greatest thinkers and teachers that humankind has produced, those ancient groundbreakers who have influenced billions of people in philosophy and spirituality, have also come to us in pairs through time and the literature of history. In ancient China, Lao Tzu, the founder of Taoist philosophy is paired with his student Chuang Tzu, just as Confucius is with Mencius. Both Lao Tzu and Confucius lived lives of relative historical obscurity and wrote relatively little that survives, but Chuang Tzu and Mencius greatly expanded and elaborated their masters' original teachings into more formal systems of thought. In ancient Greece, Socrates, considered the father of Western philosophy, wrote nothing that survives, if he wrote anything at all. Everything we know about Socrates comes primarily from his student, Plato, and a few others.

Chinese tradition even tells that Lao Tzu, refused to write any of his teachings down until the very end of his public life for fear that the written word would quickly solidify into formal dogma. This concept is echoed in Hebrew Law, which forbids the creation of any graven image of Yahweh God for the same reason: that the image itself and not the God behind the image would quickly begin to be worshipped.

Each great teacher was able to deal with philosophy and spirituality in its purest form, a form that resisted direct transmission and communication to others because of its highly experiential nature: in essence, they were calling people to a new way of experiencing life and spirit rather than persuading them to a set of beliefs. Confucius saw himself as a "transmitter who invented nothing," inviting his students only to think deeply for themselves and rigorously study the world around them; likewise, the Chinese word *tao* from the teachings of Lao Tzu is most literally translated "the way," and carries much the same connotation as Yeshua's teaching of the Way.

But if these great teachers were able to work almost exclusively in the micro, directly modeling the experiential nature of their beliefs and communicating in verbal form to small numbers of students, their disciples in ensuing generations had no such luxury. Where the master taught in pure form, person to person and heart to heart, the disciple to whom the master's torch was passed was left dealing with larger, more organized groups and had to interpret, adapt, and formalize the original teachings to fit the realities of complex macro relationships.

What Lao Tzu feared was then realized as the original, fluid teachings of the masters that were designed only to point toward truth, coalesced and solidified into formal written systems and dogma that eventually became seen as truth itself.

This is the danger of looking at these master-disciple pairs that come down through history as the dual generators of a single message, of thinking that they spoke with one voice or spoke to the same issues and within the same context. History links them as the most prominent founders of a philosophy or religion, but with the exception of a Plato, who physically studied at the feet of Socrates, the great disciple generally came later, often generations later, picking up the torch of his master in a different world, with a different audience and different demands.

Rather than standing together and speaking with one voice to all the same issues, the master-disciple pair represents stages of growth in a philosophy or religion, like growth rings in a tree: the master at the innermost ring of the sapling stage, dealing with fragile beginnings, breaking new ground with the roots of a new line of thought and spirituality. Moving further out from center, the disciple stands at a more mature stage when the tree is larger and already has many individuals using it for shelter. In other words, while the master is concerned with conceptualizing and modeling a new message, the disciple inherits the task of *applying* the message to the needs of all who have come to shelter within its branches. If the disciple is true, the original message will still shine through its application, but even so, the application of a message is not the message itself; that which points to truth is not truth itself. We have to discern the difference between the two if we are to avoid worshipping the image and not the God behind the image.

☽ ☾ ⊕ ⊕ ⊘

There is a strong parallel here to Yeshua and the great bearer of his torch into succeeding generations: Saul of Tarsus, or Paul. The New Testament is largely the story of Yeshua and Paul, with the teaching of Yeshua and the theology of Paul forming the backbone of the Christian faith. In church history, the importance of Paul's transition from the Jewish world to that of the Gentile is perhaps symbolized in the book of Acts when his original Hebrew name, *Sha'ul*, or Saul as we have it; is changed to *Paulus*, a fully Romanized name. And just as symbolically, the first Hebrew letter of *Sha'ul* is *shin*, which literally means "teeth," while the first Hebrew letter of Paul is *pey*, which means "mouth." *Sha'ul*, the one who snarls and bites as he initially persecutes Yeshua's Jewish followers, is transformed into Paulus, the one who speaks for Yeshua to a Gentile world.

If Yeshua wrote anything down, there is no evidence of it. One can easily imagine him, like Lao Tzu, no more willing to create graven images of his own words than of Yahweh God himself. As his whole mission was focused on stripping away anything that stood between the people and their God, it's no surprise that everything recorded of Yeshua in the gospels and the rest of the New Testament comes from the pens of others. Yeshua's Way of Kingdom pointed experientially to Truth and Life as he lived and breathed among his followers—showing them the Way as much as, or more than, talking about it.

Paul, on the other hand, was dealing with rapidly growing groups of followers organized into *ecclesia*, "gatherings" or "assemblies," scattered throughout the northeastern Mediterranean basin, what is today Turkey and Greece. At this stage, some fifteen to thirty years after the crucifixion, Paul needed not only to spread the message, he had to *preserve* the message against many different and competing interpretations of Yeshua's meaning and purpose, including the laws and ritual practices of Judaism itself. He had to sustain the continuation and growth of many different groups of followers and maintain their balance—culturally, politically, theologically, interpersonally—and he had to do all this often from a distance, while he was traveling from group to group, which meant he had to do it in *writing*.

Yeshua had no such tasks to deal with; in fact, there's a good case to be made that he never intended to establish a formal church outside of Judaism at all. He was fully focused on living his Way with the people in his path, using the word we translate as "church" only twice in all the gospels—and the word he used, *idta* in Aramaic and *ecclesia* in Greek, primarily means a called-out group of people—an assembly or gathering. In both cases, Matthew 16 and 18, when instructing his followers on how to deal with an errant person in the group and when praising Simon Peter for his personal revelation from God, Yeshua seems to be speaking more about his present gathering of followers than a future church as we understand that term. By contrast, that same Greek word for church, *ecclesia*, is used over seventy times in the rest of the New Testament from Acts to Revelation. Obviously, a new reality on the ground had quickly set in as Yeshua's followers grew and coalesced into more formal and non-Jewish congregations.

Where Yeshua dealt with one culture (Jewish) and one worldview (Eastern) and one context for his message (the micro relationship), Paul found himself straddling two cultures, two worldviews, and two contexts. Paul personally presided over the collision of Jewish and Gentile cultures and Eastern and Western worldviews as Yeshua's message transitioned from its Jewish roots to a Gentile tree. Then as local congregations grew in size and number, his work with individuals and small groups in micro settings had to give way to increasing work with larger macro groups, often accomplished through his letters or subordinates such as Barnabas, Silas, John Mark, Timothy, and Titus. Paul's task was extremely complex and increasingly confrontational as he brought an Eastern, Jewish, micro message to a Western, Gentile, macro, and largely hostile empire.

To understand Paul's writing, and that of other New Testament writers, is to understand the audience he was addressing, the world in which that audience lived, and the medium through which he communicated. Once again, it's all about context and original intent, and in Paul's case, this is even more pointed because all his writings come to us in the form of personal and congregational letters or epistles.

Letters are always written to a specific person or group with a specific purpose or occasion in mind, but this is even more pointed in the ancient world, where few people could read and write and writing materials were extremely scarce—difficult and expensive to produce. "Paper" was made of either specially prepared animal skins or woven strips of reeds called papyrus; inks were also laboriously made from solutions of charcoal, plant extracts, minerals, and even animal secretions. To write, produce, and deliver a letter in the ancient world was an expensive undertaking, and was only done when absolutely necessary, when specific situations or issues required special communication.

All of Paul's letters and the other letters in the New Testament carry this same intent and purpose and were not casually sent, but were a reaction to some need. There was always a reason for the letter to be written, usually an urgent one: an emergency or a critical issue or question that needed correction or clarification before a personal visit was possible. One commentator created the perfect analogy for the epistles of the New Testament, when he said they are a lot like a Jeopardy game in which you get the answers but not the questions. That's it exactly. We're reading someone else's mail: Paul's letters preserve his reactions, answers, solutions, and instructions regarding specific questions or problems, but not the problems or questions themselves. There was no need for Paul to restate them; everyone knew what they were. All he had to do was address them. Biblical scholars have spent lifetimes digging like forensic detectives through ancient literature and archeological finds to uncover what specific conditions, issues, and concerns gave occasion to Paul's letters and those of the other New Testament writers.

Why is this so important? Because...

> An answer only makes sense within the context of its
> question. Or, the question outlines the box, provides
> the parameters, within which the answer is "true."

Playing the Jeopardy game, an answer such as, "Anyone under the age of twenty-one is not permitted to drink; it is unlawful," is only true, only makes sense, if we know the question included the phrase "alcoholic beverages." Without knowing the question, we have no way of knowing how the answer is being applied—and no way of knowing whether that application may also be a valid answer to another question we may have. If we're going to make Paul's theology and instruction the basis of our faith and life as a church, we need to know exactly why he said what he said and in what way those sayings were true then, and may be "true" for us today.

There is a principle of hermeneutics, the methodology of Scriptural interpretation that all responsible scholars employ, which differentiates between "prescriptive" and "descriptive" commands. Prescriptive commands are those that *prescribe* a truth or an action across all barriers of culture, time, and geography—they always hold, and we are always beholden to them. The Golden Rule is an example of a prescriptive command, since doing to others that which you would have them do to you is always an expression of love.

A descriptive command, on the other hand, merely *describes* a practice or action that occurred at a particular place and time. In the Old Testament, Exodus 21 and Leviticus 25 spell out rules for slavery, which is clearly permitted; Israelites are allowed to enslave people from surrounding nations, buy and hold Hebrew slaves for a period of six years, and even sell their daughters into slavery. Also in these two books, the punishment of death was mandated for anything from blaspheming God's name, adultery, incest, sex with in-laws, homosexuality, and bestiality to cursing one's parents or working on the Sabbath. Evidence suggests that even the ancient Jews themselves rarely carried out such capital punishments, and today, we virtually all understand these commands and punishments not only as descriptive and non-binding, but actually immoral—the product of another world that doesn't, and shouldn't, exist today.

In the New Testament, Paul's instructions in 1 Corinthians and 1 Timothy for slaves to remain slaves or for women to keep their heads covered and remain silent during church meetings and never exhibit leadership over men are widely considered descriptive in that they may not have relevance or force in other cultures and times.

Paul's instruction in 1 Timothy for him to take a little wine with his meals to settle his stomach would probably be considered descriptive by just about everyone...especially those who believe drinking alcohol is a sin. If only all passages were as easy to interpret as this one. I grew up in a church where women had to pin Kleenex tissues on their heads before entering the building if they forgot hats or scarves. While this still may be considered a beautiful expression of modesty and submission, in Paul's world, a woman in public without a head covering was culturally like a woman today going out topless: but most church gatherings were held in people's homes, and a woman didn't have to cover her head in her own home, but was that public or private space when the group arrived? Again, the question and context provides the parameters within which the answer is true.

In his quest to strip away everything that stands between us and Kingdom, Yeshua is calling us to interpret Scripture, religious leaders and practice, and even his own teaching with discernment. The last chapter of the Sermon on the Mount, Matthew 7, is all about seeing the Way to Kingdom clearly and not being distracted or deceived. He shows us the difference between a true and false prophet and between doing good works in God's name and actually knowing God. He graphically lays out the difference between judging as condemnation, which we should not do, and discerning between those things that have the power to preserve life and those that do not—which we *must* do.

Yeshua makes the distinction between stones and loaves, fish and snakes, and warns against wolves in sheep's clothing. In ancient Israel, the round, smooth stones that were common in the country-side resembled the round, smooth loaves of bread that were traditionally baked; a fish could resemble the poisonous water snakes in the lakes and streams; and a wolf in sheep's clothing was the height of visual deception—and a pointed warning against the teaching and practice of the Pharisees whose outer garment, the *talith*, was traditionally made of pure wool or actual sheepskin.

Though these objects may look the same, especially from a distance, one has the power to sustain and preserve life while the other does not, or may actually have the power to take it away. Considering true Unity with God in Kingdom (the message) as opposed to religious forms, creeds, theologies, and cultural practices (the application of God's message), it is the same: the message has the power to bring new life, but the application may not—or may take it away.

If we blindly follow a concept or command without considering the reason for its presence in Scripture, then, as with the Oral Law of the Pharisees, we end up, not with more love or Kingdom in our midst, but just more and more oppressive law standing between us and our God.

☉ ⊙ ⊕ ⊕ ⊘

Human groups and organizations tend to move from simple to complex as they grow, and the church is no exception. Starting with the simple and straightforward Way of Yeshua, the problems, questions, and issues raised in each new congregation caused Paul and other early church leaders to react with new teachings, rules, and regulations. Yeshua never set forth a formal creed or theology, but church leaders were forced to set out ever more specific and complex creeds and theological statements if only to differentiate themselves from all the other statements of faith and theological ideas that began proliferating in the decades after Yeshua.

In the clash between cultures, worldviews, and religious ideas, the overarching issue facing the first generations after Yeshua was defining exactly what it meant to be a Follower of the Way, and their writings reflect this preoccupation—for good reason. In the face of Roman persecution, such a definition could literally mean the difference between life and painful death. And in the face of Jewish followers who believed that even Gentiles must be Jews first and keep Torah to the letter, or charismatic teachers and "prophets" with their mysterious and often wildly esoteric interpretations, or even just the normal pressures of life and the passage of time, more and more specific application: descriptive commands and guidance had to be written to ensure survival of the fledgling movement of followers.

And so, over the course of three hundred years, a simple Way of life and the spoken Good News about the unchanging love of God became a creed, a gospel, a catechism, a society, a culture, a government, a law, a theology, and eventually a canon and state religion with the power and the will to excommunicate or kill those who didn't meet basic criteria.

The New Testament records Yeshua's original message as well as the application of that message by the first few generations of his followers—people inspired by Yeshua and the Father to write books and letters full of that inspiration. But the application of a message is not the message itself; the message of Yeshua is prescriptive and unchanging—any application of it is only descriptive by definition, by virtue of its being applied to specific, temporal circumstances. If current circumstances are the same as the ancient ones, then the ancient applications can still apply, but disciples in every generation must always reapply the original message to their own world and culture and the issues they face. It is the message that is unchanging, not its application.

Leonard Sweet, in his book *Aqua Church*, makes the distinction between the content and the container:

> The mystery of the gospel is this: It is always the same (content) and it is always changing (containers). In fact, one of the ways you know the old, old truths are true is their ability to assume amazing and unfamiliar shapes while remaining themselves and without compromising their integrity.

Like water, which takes the shape of any container into which it is poured, the message of Yeshua must be poured into the shape of the lives and times of each follower and the world in which he or she lives. Just as the nature of water is not changed by the shape of the container that holds it, the nature of Yeshua's message remains equally unchanged by our containers, our applications—as long as it really is Yeshua's content that we are containing. And if we persevere and are true to the original message, it is actually *our* nature and the shape of our container that will change to fit Yeshua's content and not the other way around.

It's here that Scripture unwraps its great, God-inspired gifts. As Paul writes in 2 Timothy, "All Scripture is inspired by God and profitable for teaching, for reproof, for correction, for training in righteousness; so that the man of God may be adequate, equipped for every good work." Reading how Paul and other great disciples "worked out their salvation in fear and trembling," struggling to make Yeshua's Way a reality in their lives, is like having them right at our side, guiding and mentoring with a warm hand on our shoulder.

This is the original Hebrew understanding and use of both Scripture and Law: they are mentors, guides, and pictures of the finished product of Kingdom, not contracts to sign or rigid rules to follow. Yeshua's message is as living and active as the God behind it and can flow into every corner of our lives in any time or culture—as long as we don't try to force it in, still frozen in the shape it had at the time the letters of the New Testament were written. If we will take this applied message, frozen in time, and hold it close long enough to let it melt, it will flow again with the same vitality in our container as it did in its original container.

As Yeshua said at Matthew 9, no one puts new wine into old wineskins that are already stretched and shaped—they'll burst every time. Yeshua's message is always new and fresh; it will always expand from the inside out and stretch us to our limits: each follower of every generation must literally pour it into his or her own skin or risk losing both container and content.

It's as if Yeshua's entire being contained a message for anyone with ears to hear. Looking up and seeing Yeshua amid the noise and details of their lives, those who would become his friends saw something that caught their eye, something of value, something beautiful. They saw a brilliance, a treasure; they saw God himself. They poured all that into their lives, and it changed them. And when Yeshua was gone, they took his message, now their message too, and wrote it down and sealed it in a bottle to preserve it and send it off to those they loved and those they wanted to love, tossing it far out into the water beyond the surf. They had no idea how far it would travel, or how long, or what sort of people may eventually hold it in their hands.

Then one day, amid the knots of kelp and driftwood along our own unimaginably distant shores, those of us who are looking for such things see something that catches our eye, something of beauty and obvious value. We take it home, clean it up, study every line and curve and color, and put it on our mantle to be reminded every day of the beautiful shape of our new bottle. But...

The message is in the bottle; it's not the bottle itself.

CHALLENGE

Scripture records both a timeless message and its application for the times; interpreting scripture is learning to reapply its message for our times.

TRADITION
*Scripture is the owners' manual for life,
a direct answer for every question.*

Playing the Scriptures

INSPIRATION

Music is much more than mere notes and bar lines
scratched on paper. But it's also less.

THE MUSIC WE HEAR AND EXPERIENCE, LOVE, AND REMEMBER IS
much greater than the sum of the intricate parts of its creation in
strings, keys, hammers, and wind or of its notation in pen and ink.
We all know that the instruments that create the sounds and the
manuscript paper that records the ideas lay mute without the
inspired soul of the musician who brings them to life. But at the
same time, when you get right down to it, music really is just a
vibration in the air. It pushes air molecules against your eardrums
for a moment, and then is gone. That simple vibration is much less
than the years of training and technology it took to create the
sound in the first place, but then again, infinitely more in the heart
of the listener.

Do you remember the first time you heard music? How it made
you feel? Made you cry or made you dance? Made you want to be
able to make those sounds yourself? But if you did begin to study,
the simple experience of vibrations against your eardrums suddenly
became a vast and complicated world of training muscle and mind
to work together, of endless practice, and the interplay between
science and art.

In that world, you couldn't look at music in the same simple and naive way you did before. You may not even have enjoyed it as much as you did before now that it lay dissected and bloodless under your microscope. But if you persisted until your muscles began remembering what your mind could now forget, you could actually begin to play without thinking about it, hear a sound in your head and put it right out into the air. You could return to that simple and naive experience of the music you were now also creating. Creator, player, and listener becoming one...*knowing* the music.

So, determined to know God in this way, in the Aramaic sense of that word: *yida*, a non-rational knowing built of long experience and familiarity—how do we take God beyond mere concepts and theology the way a master musician takes music beyond mere notes and bar lines to the pure experience of beautiful vibrations in the air?

Using our common sense as the bridge, a first step is to realize, say out loud even, that the notes and bar lines of a page of music manuscript are not the music itself. They're a record of a performance or an idea. They're a frozen expression of a musical experience reduced to a code, a language, and preserved for the moment an inspired musician lifts them back off the page and recreates them in the air. Recreates them similarly, but not exactly the same. No two musical performances are ever exactly the same as some of the inspiration of the musician who plays the notes is always mixed with the inspiration of the composer who wrote the notes to change them, make them live uniquely in the air for that moment. The written music is a carrier, a conduit through which the inspiration of composer and performer are merged and re-experienced time after time.

Just as our written music is not the music itself, our sacred writings about God are not God himself. And though that analogy may seem fairly self-evident, the downstream implications may not...

An inspired composer hears a sound in her head and notates it on paper so that inspired performers can later reproduce that same sound in their own unique way. Men and women inspired by knowing God and God's knowing of them, notate their experiences of God's presence in their personal lives and the life of their communities so that others, in the throes of their own inspiration, can later reproduce that same experience of God's action in their own lives. The inspiration of the reader gets mixed in with the inspiration of the writer as the reader "plays" the text. The paper and ink of Scripture are the conduit through which God's inspiration flows from writer to reader and back to God—they are of God, but not God themselves. We re-experience God and know him better each time we read and perform the truths revealed by God to the inspired authors of Scripture.

And that's what is really at issue: revelation. Inspired people are people who have had something revealed to them. Something wonderful. Something important. Life changing. They shout "eureka." They smile a little too broadly and talk much too fast. They know something through their experience that is greater than the sum of their intellect. But rather than asking how we move beyond mere theology and intellectual understanding, the more relevant question to ask is how we go about getting this revelation, this experience of God that tells us something about him we wouldn't otherwise know.

◐ ◑ ⊕ ⊕ ⊘

There's a kind of spiritual revelation you can get from observing nature—called General Revelation—and then there's the kind you can only get downloaded directly from God—Special Revelation. Observing nature can lead you to a personal belief in God, so you can say along with Abraham Lincoln, "I can see how it might be possible for a man to look down upon the earth and be an atheist, but I cannot conceive how he could look up into the heavens and say there is no God." (Cosmological Argument.) Or with Voltaire, "If a watch proves the existence of a watchmaker, but the universe does not prove the existence of a Great Architect, then I consent to be called a fool." (Teleological Argument.)

So through general revelation, we can develop a belief in God, but from that alone, we can't intimately know, *yida*, him very well. We may be able to say through nature that God is certainly powerful and creative; we can even say that he appreciates beauty and order, but in the deepest recesses of our humanity, all that misses the point.

Albert Einstein was once asked what he believed was the most important question his work in physics could answer. He responded, "Whether the universe is a friendly place or not." That's it. Is the universe "friendly?" Is God friendly? Does he know me personally? Does he care what happens to me? Am I going to be alright? These are the questions we really want answered, and nature and General Revelation aren't much help here. Until we can answer these questions affirmatively, until we actually trust that our God is a friendly God, we're stuck—we get no further along the Way. And since looking at nature doesn't get us there, we need God to speak and tell us directly how it is.

From the very beginning of humanity, direct communication with God has always come in the non-rational form of dreams, visions, prophetic utterances, words of knowledge, prayer, and miracles. But in the modern West, rational science has explained the wind out of the sails of most of such mystical experience to the point where many of us, even the religious among us, don't believe in such special revelation anymore, claiming such "speaking" by God ended with the prophet Malachi in the last Old Testament book, or with the Apostles in the last New Testament book. That since then, we have only the Scriptures to guide us, and anything further God has to say is said from the text—that all we need is there in the book, the manual. *Sola scriptura*, scripture alone, as the Protestant Reformers cried five hundred years ago.

And even where this position isn't stated explicitly, there's often still the general assumption that the Scriptures are the true source of Special Revelation about God, and other forms of communication are suspect.

If that is true, then how should we react when the revelation from Scripture seems to contradict itself about what we already think we know about God? What do we really know about God's character when in one passage of the Scriptures we are told God will never leave us or forsake us, yet both David from the psalms and Yeshua from the cross wail, *eli, eli, lama, sabachthani*—my God, my God, why have you forsaken me? Or when we are told God is the same yesterday, today and forever then read that though his yoke is easy and his burden light, he will also visit the sins of fathers on the children and the children's children to the third and fourth generations? What do we make of God's ethics when he orders genocide, the slaughter of every inhabitant of certain ancient city-states down to the last man, woman, child, and suckling infant? When we read that God is love personified, why do we also read that he struck a man dead who merely held out his hand to steady the Ark of the Covenant as it was being transported over uneven ground?

Scholars who believe in direct and divine inspiration of the actual text of Scripture have tried to resolve these seeming contradictions as best they can, even to the point of justifying God's genocide by saying there are really no innocent victims in light of original sin. They have argued that even suckling infants are born guilty and separated from God, or that the infants God ordered to be killed were going to grow up to be as corrupt and apostate as their home culture, so without hope of redemption God was merely cutting them off at the root. Or, as the chosen people, conquering Hebrews needed to be kept ethnically and religiously pure in their promised land, so it was necessary to remove the threat of defiling intermarriage and cross cultural exchange, which in turn made those necessary ends justify God's extreme means. But such arguments only serve to beg more questions about God's character and the nature of any relationship with him—existential questions that deepen our insecurity as human beings.

From a different inspirational perspective, we can argue along with Marcus Borg that, "The Bible is a human product: it tells us how our religious ancestors saw things, not how God sees things." In other words, God inspired the *writers* of Scripture and not the words themselves. The authors, under the inspiration of their relationship with God, wrote of the experience of that relationship with their current knowledge of grammar and syntax, history, science, and culture. They were free to express themselves through the eyes of their own worldview—and in the worldview of the ancient Hebrews who wrote our Scriptures, God was the primary mover in everything that took place in their lives both individually and collectively as a nation. Whether crops failed or succeeded, children lived or died, battles were won or lost, such events were always the result of God's will and direct action. If something happened a certain way, if an army slaughtered every last man, woman, child, and suckling infant in a town, it was because God willed it, ordered it to happen that way—because it *did* happen that way and for no other reason.

We can argue this convincingly as well. We can show how the textual evidence supports the argument: that the syntax and grammar of various passages between and even within books of the Bible show huge variation and levels of linguistic style and mastery; that there is an evolution of Jewish thought from the earliest books to the latest showing differences in concepts of afterlife and ethics and ritual practice. We can argue this and that, and as we do, if we're not too immersed in our own assumptions, we eventually begin to see that we're no longer arguing over what we believe about God, but merely what we believe about Scripture—as if they are one and the same. Whether God inspired each individual word or each individual writer is an interesting conversation that has nothing to do with what we really need to know: God's nature and character and relationship with us.

Depending on our beliefs about the inspiration of Scripture, we will convince ourselves of one conclusion or another, but to what effect? From Marcus Borg again, "The spoken word is perhaps the least effective way of reaching the heart; one must constantly pay attention with one's mind. The spoken word tends to go to our heads, not our hearts." When God's revelation comes down to an argument won or lost, it would seem we've already missed the entire point of our lives of faith.

The writings of both testaments of Judeo-Christian scriptures depict a world in which God's direct revelation and communication appear to be a daily reality. The appearances of God's messengers and conversations, even bargaining with God are related in concrete, matter of fact terms. God speaks through dreams and visions and gives direct guidance for specific circumstances both verbally and through natural and supernatural occurrences from burning bushes to pillars of cloud and fire to stars. Paul speaks of gifts of the spirit that include spiritual messages of wisdom, knowledge, prophecy, discernment, and gifts of faith, healing, miracles, and speaking in different tongues. Characteristically, he lists these gifts as if they were a daily reality in the various communities in which he taught. (1 Corinthians 12)

What do we believe is our daily reality today? Do we believe that direct revelation from God is possible? We spend time in worship and prayer in order to connect with God, and many of us speak about words and gifts being received. But many others don't believe in the charisms, spiritual gifts anymore: those also ended with the last Apostle. But even in the West, the church all the way up through the Enlightenment and Reformation had a rich mystical tradition, a tradition that still continues unabated in Catholic and Orthodox circles. Now, there's that word again: *mystical, mystic, mysticism.* It's gotten a bad reputation and connotation, being now popularly intertwined with non-Christian or occult elements, but a mystic is simply someone who believes in and practices direct, non-rational experience and communication with God herenow. Understood this way, most theists are mystics—at least those of us sitting somewhere short of Deism: the belief that God wound up the universe, then left it and us to sort it all out for ourselves.

But even as we pray and worship, we often place so much emphasis on the words of Scripture alone, that the other forms of Special Revelation scripture relates are atrophying in our lives. Where did the Scriptures come from in the first place? Before there was Scripture alone, there was Special Revelation alone. Before the sacred books of Scripture were written, there were just people in direct communication with God, having mystical experiences: dreams, visions, prophecies, and miracles. It was from these direct experiences of God that God-inspired, God-breathed people wrote...*Scripture.* And they saw those writings as living and active— containing the ability to create more Special Revelation, more direct communication, mystical dreams and visions and prophecies and miracles in the lives of the people who read them and took them to heart.

Everything we can't know about God from simple observation of nature can only come from God himself in the direct communication that is possible between us as we read Scripture and live Scripture-inspired lives. Once communicated, once breathed into us, we now have something to talk about, to write about ourselves. And once we are God-breathed, we are inspired, and our writings and speakings will also be inspired. Just as inspired as Scripture? Possibly. Without the authority? Certainly. And subject to the checks and balances that Scripture provides? Absolutely. But inspired? Surely.

Until we vigorously pursue a full life of Special Revelation, look in all the directions from which God speaks, the reading of Scripture remains only hearsay, a third person experience until we make it first person in the day by day following, in the exercise of our own mystical prayer and relational life, mixing our inspiration with that of inspired authors. To move from mere understanding to *yida*-knowing is the goal: to hear God's voice daily, to learn to trust that voice even when it comes from unexpected places. The Scriptures are one tool God uses. But Scripture tells us there are others, if we give ourselves permission to use them.

When the student is ready, the teacher appears.

When we are ready as students, everything and everyone can teach us. When we are ready as students, we will be tuned to see truth wherever it appears, and not just where we expect to find it. We will begin to see God as the primary mover in every aspect of our lives, and it will change the way we see and hear and how we express ourselves. A favorite expression of Yeshua, was, "He who has ears, let him hear." It was his call for all of us to experience truth from an unexpected place, from an unexpected voice, in an unexpected way: to move to a new vista, a new point of connection and inspiration, to dream dreams and prayerfully see visions and miracles in every detail of life.

Are we ready to graduate from our heads to our hearts, from merely appreciating the beauty of creation to actually hearing the music of God's voice playing through it? Through each of us? To join in the playing is to move from third person to first and realize that the music isn't scratched and frozen on the page, it's as liquid and living in the air we breathe as we are willing to join in the vibration.

From Thomas Merton...

"...the Lord plays and diverts Himself in the garden of His creation, and if we could let go of our own obsession with what we think is the meaning of it all, we might be able to hear His call and follow Him in the mysterious cosmic dance. We do not have to go very far to catch the echoes of that game, and of that dancing. When we are alone on a starlit night, when by chance we see the migrating birds in autumn descending on a grove of junipers to rest and eat, when we see children in a moment when they are really children, when we know love in our own hearts...at such times the awakening, the turning inside out of all values, the 'newness,' the emptiness and the purity of the vision that make themselves evident, provide a glimpse of the cosmic dance.

For the world and time are the dance of the Lord in emptiness. The more we persist in misunderstanding the phenomena of life, the more we analyze them out into strange finalities and complex purposes of our own, the more we involve ourselves in sadness, absurdity, and despair. But it does not matter much, because no despair of ours can alter the reality of things, or stain the joy of the cosmic dance which is always there. Indeed, we are in the midst of it, and it is in the midst of us, for it beats in our very blood, whether we want it to or not.

Yet the fact remains that we are invited to forget ourselves on purpose, cast our awful solemnity to the winds and join the general dance."

CHALLENGE

*Scripture is the record of an intentional relationship with God,
inspiring us to live ours with the same intention and abandon.*

TRADITION
*Without faith it is impossible to please God;
faith is our power over brokenness and doubt.*

Creatures of a Broken Heart

VULNERABILITY

> Now that you have emerged from your narrow sphere and have
> seen the great ocean, you know your own insignificance,
> and I can speak to you of great principles.
> *Chuang Tzu*

IN A SHORT PIECE CALLED "AUTUMN FLOODS," WRITTEN PROBABLY
in the third century BCE, Chuang Tzu tells the story of the spirit
of a river whose ego swells with the swelling of his banks at the
time of the autumn floods in ancient China:

> It was the time of autumn floods. Every stream poured into
> the river, which swelled in its turbid course. The banks receded
> so far from one another that it was impossible to tell a cow
> from a horse.
>
> Then the Spirit of the River laughed for joy that all the beauty
> of the earth was gathered to himself. Down with the stream he
> journeyed east, until he reached the ocean. There, looking east-
> wards and seeing no limit to its waves, his countenance changed.
> And as he gazed over the expanse, he sighed and said to the Spir-
> it of the Ocean, "A vulgar proverb says that he who has heard
> but part of the truth thinks no one equal to himself. And such a
> one am I."

It's fascinating how the moment of our greatest personal fullness is also the moment of our greatest self-deception. Believing that whatever part of the truth we have is all the truth there is, really is a dangerous thing, a roadblock to further progress. But in running the course of his relatively narrow canal and suddenly emptying out into the sea of his own insignificance, the River experienced a moment of rebirth, a moment containing all the disorientation and disquiet of the newborn infant as he found himself suddenly thrust into unfamiliar territory of frightening proportions.

How traumatic is it to be born into this world, to be violently expelled from warmth and safety, to flail about in the cold with no reassuring boundaries? Thankfully, none of us can remember. But what the newborn may experience as the end of significance and fullness, we later recognize as the beginning of new adventure and exhilaration, one based on much larger scope and perspective, one containing a bigger bite of truth.

As long as we remain in the womb, we may feel secure, but there is only so much growth, so much truth that can be experienced there. As long as we remain in the womb, we remain ignorant of anything that may exist outside the sound of our mother's heartbeat, of any truth that doesn't flow directly through our umbilical tether. That this wrenching process of rebirth is absolutely essential, that it is the only Way to Truth and Life and the Father's love, is beautifully expressed in the Ocean's first words to the River when he says,

"You cannot speak of ocean to a well-frog, the creature of a narrower sphere. You cannot speak of ice to a summer insect, the creature of a season." And following the direct line of Chuang Tzu's thought, I would ask:

> How do you speak of perfect love to a human being,
> the creature of a broken heart?

◌ ◌ ◌ ◌ ◌

"Life is difficult." The opening line of M. Scott Peck's classic book, *The Road Less Traveled*, underscores our brokenness and broken-heartedness as humans. No one gets out of childhood unscathed, though some are certainly more traumatized than others, and life continues to be difficult as we transition into young adulthood and for as long as we're breathing. The author's point was that even though it is difficult, a never-ending series of problems to solve, once we accept life on its own difficult terms, the fact that it's difficult won't matter anymore. And as true as that is, acceptance like that doesn't come easy or cheap. In the midst of the pain, it's very hard to see how our repeated experience of the loss of safety and significance can possibly be a normal part of life, let alone a rebirth and the only possibility for growth and a bigger bite of truth.

Carrying on like walking wounded, the difficulties of life have repeatedly broken our hearts and often our spirits. Our experience of life is that people are not reliable, that their love is conditional and capricious, that to love is to become vulnerable to the unreliable love of others: to be hurt, to be hurt badly, to vow never to put ourselves in such a position again, and to guard ourselves every step of the way before we do.

Our insecurities are betrayed in the textbook dance between codependent lovers in which one advances while the other retreats until "caught," only to have the one who was advancing begin to retreat with the other chasing after. Back and forth the lovers retreat and advance on each other, moving "forward" together in parallel tracks, never really getting any closer—but not any farther apart either.

Afraid to be alone, but equally afraid to open up and bare our vulnerable spots, our broken hearts envelope us like the womb, creating a self-contained universe in which the truth of our hurt becomes all the truth there is. We live bounded by the limitations of our deepest fears that hold us just as surely as the walls of the frog's well or the life span of the insect. And whether we can articulate it or not, we are always searching for a way to start over, to fix and forget what was broken, targeting anything in our paths that seems to promise the security and fullness we somehow remember and have to believe can exist for us again.

But Yeshua is telling us that there is only one source of this new beginning, and until we accept it, all our other targets will only drive the knife deeper. How do we ever hope to accept the perfect love that Yeshua offers—a love we may never have experienced or seen, a love that we don't even know exists outside our wells? How do we escape the confines of our broken hearts long enough to even glimpse the ocean of God's love?

It's easy to say that the answer is faith and to quote Hebrews 11:6: "Without faith it is impossible to please God, for he who comes to God must believe that he is and that he is a rewarder of those who seek him."

I'm not sure I can count how many times I've heard this verse recited as a cure-all to a hurting or depressed person and sometimes as a reprimand for even the most casual expression of doubt about any life situation from finances to health to wondering whether there's enough gas in the tank to get home. But this is a misuse of the passage and a misunderstanding of the meaning of faith.

Faith is not the end of doubt; faith is the beginning of trust.

Can we have faith and still have doubt? Of course. Can we have courage and still have fear? Faith is not measured by the absence of doubt any more than courage is measured by the absence of fear. Faith and courage are *defined by* and can exist only in the *presence of* doubt and fear, and they are measured by the action taken in spite of the presence of doubt and fear.

Faith is acting as if there were no doubt just as courage is acting as if there were no fear. It's in the action itself that doubts and fears slowly begin to dissipate in the experience of trust gained along the Way. Faith is not passive certainty; courage doesn't sit on the shelf next to a folded flag or a medal—they exist only in motion.

The Way of Yeshua is essentially the Way to trust.

In Aramaic, faith, *haimanuta*, is a form of *etamen*, believe, and both words mean the confidence that includes our concepts of belief (idea), faith, (action), and trust, (experience) all at the same time. "Without faith it is impossible to please God" literally means that without faith (repeated action) that leads to trust (accumulated experience) it is impossible to enter into the pleasure (will, desire, deepest purpose) of God. And coming to God by believing (faith + trust), literally means to have learned through repeated experience to trust who he really is, what he really is. Seeking God is its own reward in the quality of life that the awareness of God's presence fosters (kingdom)—no waiting for heaven in order to collect.

This process of belief-faith-trust is just that: a process and not an event. The process *begins* with an event, a first step that allows us to take the next step and all the steps after, but it's still a process, and each event only a single step. But the first step is the hardest; the first step is prerequisite. It may be a truism to say that without the first step taken, no other steps are possible, but this first step is not just the first step in a series, it defines the ground on which, the atmosphere in which, all other steps live and breathe.

Yeshua's saying that knowing truth will make you free is a declaration of this first step. The Aramaic word *serara*, at its root means *that which opens possibilities*—implying that this first step creates the very possibility of rebirth and transformation where it didn't exist before. It's the step that recognizes truth. What truth? The truth of gospel? The Good News that God's love is free? Yes. But because

God's love is free and can't be earned or controlled, there is a related and devastating truth about ourselves that we must face if we are ever to take this crucial first step toward freedom from our fears.

Over the last fifteen plus years, as I've been working with people in the area of recovery from alcohol and drug addiction, I've grown to love and greatly respect the Twelve Steps of Alcoholics Anonymous. As I began this work, I approached the Twelve Steps with an existing appreciation for their long history of success in bringing addicted people into full and lasting sobriety, but I was unprepared to discover just how universal the Steps are for each and every one of us.

We are *all* recovering from something.

We are all recovering from the broken heart each one of us received as we left the garden of our childhood at whatever age that was—and every broken heart since. For most of us, that recovery is arrested, but whether we've begun the process of recovery or not, until we return to the garden, to Kingdom, until the hurt is finally put to rest, we are forced to mask it, to bandage and anesthetize it as best we can in order to survive.

Some of us mask our broken hearts with alcohol and drugs; others with sex or obsession with our work. Some of us give up and drop out while others strive for achievement and power. Some of us join churches and become fanatic about our faith or leave churches and become fanatic about political or social causes—or both at the same time. Some of us become thrill-seekers, adrenaline junkies, and others become recluses. We obsess over our possessions or our sports teams or the lives of celebrities who represent for us all that we believe would relieve our pain: beauty, power, wealth, adoration. Some of us become angry and others depressed; some become violent and others suicidal, but all of us are participating in the same behavior: the masking of the fear that comes from a broken heart.

I often tell recovering addicts that in the larger view of life, they are really more fortunate than many of us. Since their addictions, their masks, are so destructive, they often bring the addict to the point of recognizing the need for their recovery much sooner than those who have engaged more socially-acceptable addictions such as obsession with work or play or church or wealth. We all need to begin our recovery, but the fear from our broken hearts is so great that we cling to our addictions like life itself, and it's not until everything falls apart and our lives become completely unmanageable that we finally begin to look for another way. Getting to that point, hitting whatever bottom is sufficient to strip away the mask of the addictions we substitute for Kingdom, is the key to the recovery process and the beginning of the Twelve Steps.

And what is the first step of the Twelve Steps?

> We admitted we were powerless over alcohol—
> that our lives had become unmanageable.

The first and crucial step to rebirth, the devastating truth about ourselves that will make us free of anything and everything that keeps us fearful and living outside Kingdom, is the realization that in the most profound way, we are completely *powerless*. And that powerlessness is not just over alcohol, but extends to every force in life outside ourselves. Intellectually, we may understand this at some level, but emotionally and psychologically, it's no easy admission. Most of us will do almost anything rather than admit the powerlessness we mistakenly equate with insignificance. And when the carefully cultivated control we believe we have over the pain in our lives is all that seems to separate us from complete breakdown and despair, it's easy to understand why so few of us ever take this first step through the narrow gate Yeshua described at Matthew 7 as the trailhead of the way to life.

Who among us gives up power voluntarily?

⊙ ⊙ ⊕ ⊕ ⊗

After bringing the Continental army to victory over the British, George Washington couldn't wait to relinquish his commission and command and go back home to his beloved Mount Vernon to resume his life as a farmer. But with the failure of the United States' first attempt at governing itself, it became obvious that a new constitution was needed along with a new leader capable of holding the people together long enough to give the new nation a chance. The only man with the universal respect and stature for the job was Washington. He was beseeched to come to New York and act as the first president of the new Union, but he wanted nothing more than to be home with his family and his land. It took him quite some time to be convinced that there really was no other way. How rare is it for a person not to seek power even when it is freely offered? To release it willingly and gracefully when the time comes?

The truth is, we admire those who acquire power, those who fight till their last breath, those who will not submit to the will of another. This attitude is so seared into the fabric of our culture, we rarely give up power or admit defeat until we are completely beaten down, completely out of other options, and have nothing left to lose. And even then, we may give up, but we don't surrender.

> Giving up is merely the end of resistance;
> surrender is the beginning of submission.

We often think that giving up and surrender are the same, but they're not—giving up may be the end of resistance against a partic-ular force in our lives, but only true surrender marks the beginning of submission. Giving up admits nothing; giving up is a tactical move that leaves us ready to fight another day, but surrender prepares us to accept the truth that life is presenting. Without true surrender, complete submission, we keep all our old fears and brokenness firmly in place behind our defenses as we hit the next bottom and the next. In the words of AA literature, "We have no enduring strength until we admit complete defeat." Without submission to and admission of the truth, there's always another bottom to hit.

And that truth is: *we have no power*. Yeshua said at Matthew 6, "Who of you by worrying can add a single hour to your life, an inch to your height?" Such basic and vital power over the smallest of things is as utterly beyond us as the power to change the weather or the course of the stars. The irony is that to admit powerlessness is not to give up any power at all; we never had any to begin with. Personal power is an illusion. Seeing that truth makes us free, because we suddenly realize we don't have to continue trying to hold on to power, to seek or pretend we have power...there isn't any.

There's a wonderful scene in the movie "The Matrix" in which a young boy is bending spoons with his mind. He hands the spoon to the hero inviting him to try as well. The boy says to him,

"Don't try to bend the spoon; that's impossible. Only try to see the truth."

"What's that?" the hero asks.

"There is no spoon."

It may be just as impossible to force ourselves to give up the power and control that we believe is our lifeline, the only thing standing between us and a padded room. But thankfully we don't have to do that. All we have to do is begin to see the truth: we have no power. All we have to do is become willing to give up the *illusion* of our power, to see ourselves as we really are—completely and utterly dependent, like children, like servants, like *talya*.

> Unless you are changed inwardly and become like young
> children (*talya*), you will not enter the Kingdom of Heaven.
> Matthew 18:3

Translated as "child," the Aramaic word *talya* means both child and domestic slave or bond servant at the same time, delivering the full meaning of Yeshua's saying. Despite all the qualities of dependence and vulnerability, the child lacks the conscious choice of submission that brings the servant to the humility of accepting powerlessness.

This is Yeshua's first step, the step without which no other steps are possible, and it's exactly the same as the first step of the Twelve Steps. To change inwardly, to change from inside out and become like children and house servants at the same time takes on new meaning now as we realize we are not changing our basic natures at all. We are only realizing and submitting to what we have been all along: powerless, dependent, and vulnerable. Power is the enabler of self-deception, and the illusion of personal power chains us to our addictions. Seeing the truth, letting it grow in us from inside out, plants us firmly on the Way to freedom from our fears.

But Yeshua doesn't stop there. The Sermon on the Mount, comprising Matthew 5, 6, and 7, contains all of Yeshua's teaching in a concise and concentrated form. The form of the Sermon is very deliberately arranged, and many scholars believe it may have been used as an early catechism of his collected sayings to teach those new in the faith. And here again, the first words out of Yeshua's mouth to begin the Sermon are: "Blessed are the poor in spirit, for theirs is the Kingdom of Heaven."

It is the first step once again. "Poor in spirit," *meskenaee b'rukh*, is an Aramaic idiom that means, humble, dependent, vulnerable, having an attitude of poverty even if rich. These people, the ones who realize who and what they really are, are the only ones who will be able to see through their need for control and embrace a love that is uncontrollable—who will be able to see that such a completely free and unconditional love could actually exist at all. Only those who know they are utterly dependent are prepared to accept that which can't be earned. There is no other Way.

Frustratingly, it takes a long time to hit enough bottoms to begin to see and accept the truth. Often it takes us to the very ends of our lives before we realize the futility of holding on to our illusions. In a melancholy but most beautiful way, Solomon, King of Israel, at the end of a long life of striving after power, wealth, and wisdom, finally admits and accepts the truth of his condition, the condition of all of us, as he writes in Ecclesiastes:

All things are wearisome... The eye is not satisfied with seeing, nor is the ear filled with hearing. That which has been is that which will be, and that which has been done is that which will be done... There is no remembrance of earlier things; and also of the later things that will occur, there will be for them no re-membrance among those who will come later still...

I set my mind to seek and explore by wisdom concerning all that has been done under heaven... I have seen all the works which have been done under the sun, and behold, all is vanity and striving after wind. What is crooked cannot be straightened and what is lacking cannot be counted.

Over the course of his long life, Solomon, like the spirit of the River, has reached the sea. As he looks out over the limitless waves with all he had gathered to himself—the unimaginable wealth, the architecture, the concubines, the kingdoms, the power of king-ship—he realizes it all means nothing in the face of the vastness of his death...

I built houses for myself, I planted vineyards for myself; I made gardens and parks for myself and I planted in them all kinds of fruit trees; I made ponds of water for myself from which to irrigate a forest of growing trees. I bought male and female slaves, and I had homeborn slaves. Also I possessed flocks and herds larger than all who preceded me in Jerusalem.

Also, I collected for myself silver and gold and the treasure of kings and provinces. I provided for myself male and female singers and the pleasures of men—many concubines. Then I became great and increased more than all who preceded me in Jerusalem. My wisdom also stood by me. All that my eyes desired I did not refuse them... Thus I considered all my activities which my hands had done and the labor which I had exerted, and behold all was vanity and striving after wind, and there was no profit under the sun.

So I turned to consider wisdom, madness, and folly... And I saw that wisdom excels folly as light excels darkness. The wise man's eyes are in his head, but the fool walks in darkness. And yet I know that one fate befalls them both.

Then I said to myself, "As is the fate of the fool, it will also befall me. Why then have I been extremely wise?" So I said to myself, "This too is vanity." For there is no lasting remembrance of the wise man as with the fool, inasmuch as in the coming days all will be forgotten. And how the wise man and the fool alike die!

> The moment of our greatest personal fullness
> is also the moment of our greatest self-deception.

When that fullness empties out into the sea and the truth is seen for the first time, we always resist at first, come kicking and screaming into the blinding light of our new reality. Such is the trauma of birth and rebirth as Solomon screams:

Vanity of vanities! All is vanity. What advantage does man have in all his work which he does under the sun? A generation goes and a generation comes, but the earth remains forever. Also, the sun rises and the sun sets; and hastening to its place it rises there again. Blowing toward the south, then turning toward the north, the wind continues swirling along; and on its circular courses the wind returns. All the rivers flow into the sea, yet the sea is not full. To the place where the rivers flow, there they flow again.

There is only one truth. Truth is universal, so the images we use to describe truth are universal as well. From the rivers of ancient Israel to those of ancient China, from the wisdom of Solomon to that of Chuang Tzu, there is a consistency of mind and heart, for as the Spirit of the Ocean continues speaking to the Spirit of the River, he says,

Now that you have emerged from your narrow sphere and have seen the great ocean, you know your own insignificance, and I can speak to you of great principles.

There is no body of water beneath the canopy of heaven which is greater than ocean. All streams pour into it without cease, yet it does not overflow. It is constantly being drained off, yet it is never empty. Spring and autumn bring no change; floods and droughts are equally unknown. And thus it is immeasurably superior to mere rivers and brooks—though I would not venture to boast on this account, for I get my shape from the universe, my vital power from yin and yang. In the universe I am but as a small stone or a small tree on a vast mountain. And conscious thus of my own insignificance, what is there of which I can boast?

The Four Seas, are they not to the universe but like puddles in a marsh? The Middle Kingdom, is it not to the surrounding ocean like a tare-seed in a granary? Of all the myriad created things, man is but one. And of all those who inhabit the land, live on the fruit of the earth, and move about in cart and boat, an individual man is but one. Is not he, as compared with all creation, but as the tip of a hair upon a horse's skin?

Solomon and the Spirit of the River are newly reborn. As all newborns, they are disoriented, dismayed, disillusioned, deflated, and frightened at the bigness of the truth they have discovered. As they now are, Ocean once was when he first had to come to terms with the limits of his illusions. But he is no longer afraid because by moving out into the vastness of his new world, he realized that terms like great and small and power and dependency ultimately have no meaning. He tells River:

> Dimensions are limitless; time is endless. Conditions are not invariable; terms are not final. Thus, the wise man looks into space, and does not regard the small as too little, nor the great as too much; for he knows that there is no limit to dimension. He looks back into the past, and does not grieve over what is far off, nor rejoice over what is near; for he knows that time is without end.
>
> He investigates fullness and decay, and does not rejoice if he succeeds, nor lament if he fails; for he knows that conditions are not invariable. He who clearly apprehends the scheme of existence, does not rejoice over life, nor repine at death; for he knows that terms are not final.

Our natural response to a broken heart is to try to cover our vulnerability with power. Assumed control over the people and circumstances of our lives gives us temporary relief from the pain, but the tools of control are the tools of illusion; they'll only take us so far, and they'll never mend our broken hearts. There is only one Way out or through, and it involves the death of our illusions and rebirth into truth. "Truly, truly, I say to you, unless one is born again he cannot see the kingdom of God," Yeshua tells Nicodemus at John 3. Yeshua is the Way, the Truth, and the Life—the only Way to Father mapped out by the process of his life, death, and resurrection, a resurrection that shows us how we really can breathe through our fears because conditions are not invariable and terms are not final.

The first step is to recognize our utter powerlessness, to let go, to be willing to start over again in complete vulnerability and dependence, a different vantage full of new sights and sounds and adventure that for all our newfound smallness is still greater than where we were before. Remember, Yeshua tells us that John the Baptist may have been the greatest of the prophets born of woman, but the least in the Kingdom is still greater than he, if only because of the realization that dimensions are limitless and terms are not final.

Vulnerability is not weakness, but the beautiful, essential recognition of limitless relationship in which measurement has no meaning. We have been made part of everything that is and has always been...are we willing to accept the powerlessness of that perfect position?

☉ ⊕ ⊕ ⊕ ⊕

I took my two-year-old son on a walk through a nature reserve near our house one Sunday afternoon. Couched way down in the sling of the stroller, he looked small and far away. All I could see of him was the wind ruffling through the fine hair on top of his head as I alternately watched the landscape and the footpath, making sure that I was guiding the wheels over the safest and smoothest route. Moving deeper into the hills, the path narrowed as mustard plants overgrew along the sides, rising chest and neck high covered with their tiny yellow flowers. I could see the path curving off, disappearing into overgrowth then reappearing farther down the hill. In the middle distance below us, there were housing tracts, the parking lot, a road alive with traffic, and with the far distant mountains as backdrop, all the familiar sights and sounds of my world aligned in a comforting glance.

The path had grown narrow enough that the stroller was now parting the mustard stalks as we pushed through, and as I looked down at my son, I realized that he had gone unnaturally quiet and still. I could sense his focus and concentration right through the top of his head and looked down the path toward what may have been holding his attention when a sudden thought struck me.

I bent way down, almost doubled over, and held my face at the same level as his, continuing to push through what magically had changed from mustard bushes to tall trees with their yellow tops high over my head. The whole scene instantly transformed from a narrow footpath on a nearby hill to a mysterious road deep in the forest; we could have been hundreds of miles from the nearest sign of anything that seemed familiar and safe. I could imagine we were traveling a hobbit road through Middle Earth, that horses with armored riders would come thundering around the next curve at any moment filling the scene with flying clumps of earth, flared nostrils, and the glint of hardened metal.

By simply lowering my position, I had left the world with which I was so familiar and comfortable and had entered a new one, the world of my child—a world viewed from only three feet off the ground where even a rutted footpath could hold any promise or possibility. I had been given just a glimpse of whatever it was my boy was seeing in all its newness and mystery, but it was enough to begin to understand.

Being reborn tears us from everything we know and think we understand. It takes from us all the comforting and familiar things we have piled up around ourselves in the effort to feel bounded and held and in control. It seems to require so much of us, so much loss, that we resist as long as we can. But rebirth doesn't take from us anything we actually possess and offers back everything we already do. If we can find our Way not to simply give up, stop resisting, but to truly surrender and take that first step, our rebirth will open the rest of the Way to immense new experience full of the adventure and exhilaration of possibilities we didn't know existed.

From the other side of his rebirth, Yeshua looks up at us from the standing height of a child, from the kneeling height of a servant at our feet, saying that what he has done, we can do, and greater things than these. There he is, way down there with the wind combing through his hair, beckoning with his broad, blinding smile and speaking with the unmistakable ring of the truth that makes us free because in all our powerlessness, there is one power we do possess— the power to choose to hitch our strollers to the power greater than ourselves, the only power that can take us where we really want to go.

As creatures of a broken heart, the truth that the Way to healing is actually down and not up, a letting go rather than an acquisition, an admission of vulnerability, a lowering of imagined position, is just too frightening to accept as long as we believe we have any power left to defend. But when the first wall comes down, and instead of the hordes of the enemy we have feared so long, we are greeted with a limitless view of ocean, we are at first still terrified with the dawning of our own seeming insignificance. But if we will stay on that shore, not run back to the fortification of womb and well, our eyes will slowly adjust to the brilliance of the light, and we will stand blinking and squinting and eventually smiling with all the other vulnerable ones who have come to know they are finally on their way home.

CHALLENGE
Faith wielded as personal power is religious illusion;
faith with power to heal broken hearts rests on powerless vulnerability.

TRADITION
*Fear of the Lord is foundational to our faith;
a healthy fear of punishment keeps us safe.*

The Suburbs of Hell

FEAR

> The doors of hell are locked on the inside.
> C.S. Lewis

I'VE BEEN SPENDING A LOT OF TIME IN THE SUBURBS OF HELL lately. As a pastor, there is never a shortage of opportunities each week: a Thursday night study, a class at a local bible college, a men's group, conversations at meals, counseling. It seems that any group of Christians talking long enough ultimately ends up in hell.

Who's in, who's out? Who's up, who's down?

What disqualifies us from God's ultimate acceptance and what ultimately saves? I've seen it time and time again over the years—this tendency to reflexively judge our lives, our faith, and each other in the light of hell.

Do we need to do this? Why are we so defensive about our ultimate acceptance by the God we characterize as all-loving? Why are we so obsessed with a concept of eternal punishment that doesn't even appear in the Old and New Testaments as we understand it?

I read a new book by one of those pastors, the ones willing to stray from the fold by pushing the theological envelope. It's in this book that he tackles the doctrine of hell...kind of a no-win situation to discuss openly, and reviews by orthodox Christians are more than predictably scathing...they are ostracizing; personally attacking author as well as text. If the goal of this author is simply to protect the good news of the Father's love, is it possible to take that good news too far? To understand God's love so broadly that we no longer believe in everlasting punishment in a lake of fire? And are yes and no our only two choices?

I'm in agreement with Shakespeare. I do believe there are more things in heaven and earth than are dreamt of in our philosophy—or theology—and that we should remain open. Sir Jonathan Sacks, chief Rabbi of the British Commonwealth, wrote, "Those who are confident of their faith are not threatened, but enlarged by the different faiths of others."

I agree with that too.

What makes us so fearful and angry? Why do we think it's appropriate to tear into each other because of our differing views of God and his interaction with us? To act unlovely in the name of God's love without any sense of the irony involved, to attempt to destroy differing voices in the name of theological unity is to deliver any Good News stillborn into our community.

So why are we so fixated on hell? Could it really be as simple as fear versus love, either living in love or living in fear? Love connects and accepts while fear is characterized by separation, division, isolation—the ancient definition of sin itself. But as fear is *realized* and *manifested* in anger, stress, depression, anxiety, envy, jealousy, covetousness, greed...then every dysfunctional human emotion and attitude, *every single one*, can trace its lineage back to fear. If fear is ground zero for everything that wrecks our lives and relationships then fear, not hate, is the opposite of love, which is why perfect love casts out fear at 1 John 4: "There is no fear in love; but perfect love casts out fear, because fear involves punishment, and the one who fears is not perfected in love." To the extent we have those negative symptoms in our lives, we have fear—and we have displaced love.

That's how we know where we stand after all. Want to get to the crux of your pain in any given moment? You can ask the same question every time...

What am I afraid of?

Not an easy question to ask. And one that will drag us through layers of resistance even as it leads like a laser-guided missile to the source of our pain.

And what are we ultimately afraid of? *Not being accepted*...both herenow in this life and therethen in whatever we understand of the next one. Dig deep enough into any one of us and you will hit the water table of a terrified child in the dark looking for a hand to hold.

John is telling us in that amazing fourth chapter of his first letter, that fear is the felt absence of love's acceptance in the same way that anxiety is the felt absence of trust...two ways of making the same point, a point the church seems to have missed based on much of its teaching. If John is right, the fear of hell's punishment, cultivated by the church over millennia and at best meant to drive us back to the safety of God's love, is a contradiction in terms. Such institutional fear used as a tool to modify our behavior as a group, can never simultaneously be an expression of mercy and acceptance for each of us as individuals. If love is the opposite of fear, and love is unity, then fear is separation—and separation is sin. You can't get to love through fear any more than you get to unity through separation. Or in John's words, to fear hell's punishment is to not be perfected in love—to have not experienced the radical completion of God's love.

The means we use must match the ends we seek.

In spiritual formation as in one-on-one relationships, the means we use must match the ends we seek. How can we work for unity without first being unified? And if that sounds like a chicken and egg paradox, ask this way: how do we work for unity while actively making divisive choices, without at least making choices to act as if we were already connected? Yeshua said like begets like, so fear and separation only breed more fear and separation, never unity and love. Unity requires a clean break with fear, a quantum leap into the unknowns of the Good News. A falling backward into the arms of something never fully understood, but more and more trusted with each falling.

We fixate on hell because we fear it. We fear that God really won't ultimately accept us—a polite euphemism for hell. We want to believe we know others are going to hell, because at least we can imagine we're better than they, which means we still have a chance. We tear into others and their differing views because they're chipping away at the carefully constructed walls of our fortress—the worldview and theology that we hope will save us from the inferno.

And if we are living in such fear, never trusting that such good news as perfect love really exists, we can never get any further away from hell than its suburbs. We will live continually in its shadow, in its smog, with its skyline always on the horizon. It's a terrible thing to live in fear. Especially when the fear is of our own choosing. Yeshua gave us an alternative; we say we've taken it, but our obsessions, our lack of civility, and our mailing address give us away.

Perfect love casts out fear. Get that and get it all.

But how? How can we even begin to leave our fears behind? Certainly not by fixating on them; that only makes them stronger. Fixating on God? Better, but if we fear him too, to fixate on God fearfully is to turn a loving Father into a talisman that we clutch like a rabbit's foot on our way past the graveyard.

We know that fear of the Lord is foundational to our faith, but we have institutionalized that phrase in the Scriptures without understanding that for the Hebrews who wrote those words, fearing God doesn't mean afraid of God—it means intimately knowing our relationship to God, with all the humble dependency, submission, respect, reverence, and awe such knowing entails. Before we can *fearlessly* fear God, we need to have spent enough time together to know the truth as Yeshua did—God as a fearless lover loving first so we can fearlessly love after. John says this straight out: we love because he first loved us (1 John 4:19), but fearless love is written all over the gospels. The Good News is *made* of fearless love, but we don't see it in a message made of words we no longer understand from a modern, Western worldview.

So we fixate on hell. We understand that alright.

But...

Consider that in the language of the Hebrews who wrote our Scriptures, there is no word that corresponds to the meaning of our word hell. In fact, Jews then and now have no set doctrine of the afterlife at all. Although they believe that death is not the end of human existence, the world to come, *olam ha-ba*, is God's domain and unknowable from human perspective. Living between heaven and earth, our job as humans is to bring heaven to earth and earth to heaven, that is, to merge the unity and connectedness of heaven with the individual form and function of earth. If we just do our job herenow, learn to see the unity of heaven in every daily detail of life and choose accordingly, then even without understanding the mechanics of the next life, we know that the absolute wisdom and compassion of God will take care of the rest. And fear subsides.

Even so, Hebrews did have words referring to the afterlife, and the Aramaic word that most closely matches our concept of hell is *gehenna*, used several times by Yeshua in the gospels. Gehenna was modeled on *ge-hinnom*, a valley immediately south of Jerusalem that seven centuries before was the site of ritual child sacrifice. By Yeshua's time, the valley was considered cursed and used only as a garbage dump where fires were kept continually burning organic waste as a method of disposal and purification against disease.

Hebrews used the valley as metaphor to conceive of how God's justice could be served in the next life for those who died without atonement in this one. But the fires of gehenna were meant to purify and preserve, not punish, just as fire and salt functioned in ancient cultures before antibiotics and refrigeration. And though the pain from the flames of gehenna was understood to be real, it was also temporary, lasting as long as needed to burn away impurities—traditionally a maximum of twelve months, allowing humans to eventually move on. Of course the number twelve was being used symbolically to mean a completed cycle, but the *kaddish*, the Jewish prayer for the dead was ritually said for eleven months for parents, because to recite it for the full twelve was to imply they were wicked enough to serve the full term.

With this fundamental difference in hand, passages such as Yeshua saying at Mark 9 that we should remove hands, feet, and eyes that cause us to stumble rather than go to gehenna—often translated *hell*—where the worm doesn't die and fire never stops, take on new meaning. The fires of gehenna are never quenched and what the fires don't burn, the worms continually eat, but for each individual, only for as long as there are impurities to cleanse. And at Luke 16, Yeshua's parable of a rich man's torment after death and his separation by an unbridgeable chasm from the beggar Lazarus's comfort at Abraham's side, would also need to be seen as impermanent.

Alternately, an ancient Hebrew folktale tells us that in *olam haba*, no one's arms bend at the elbows. Those who are in hell are starving to death because they can't reach their mouths to feed themselves, while those who are in heaven have learned to feed each other. In this view, heaven and hell aren't places we go or are placed by God, they are states of spiritual enlightenment that allow us to see more or less of God's true nature.

Were the Hebrews right about hell? This would be the wrong way to phrase the question since Jews would claim to know nothing certain about God's domain. But what is certain is that those who wrote the words of our Scriptures and those who listened to the words falling from Yeshua's lips conceived afterlife quite differently than we do considering the words that we have used to translate them.

Most importantly, the Jews who wrote our Scriptures didn't fear hell; they feared God. And because they didn't fear hell, their fear of God could be healthy and trusting.

Thinking along these same lines, C.S. Lewis wrote in *The Problem of Pain*:

> "The doors of hell are locked on the inside. I do not mean that the ghosts may not wish to come out of Hell, in the vague fashion wherein an envious man 'wishes' to be happy: but they certainly do not will even the first preliminary stages of that self-abandonment through which alone the soul can reach any good. They enjoy forever the horrible freedom they have demanded, and are therefore self-enslaved: just as the blessed, forever submitting to obedience, become through all eternity more and more free."

In *The Great Divorce*:

> "There are only two kinds of people in the end: those who say to God, 'Thy will be done' and those to whom God says, in the end, '*Thy* will be done.' All that are in hell choose it. Without that self-choice, there could be no hell. No soul that seriously and constantly desires joy will ever miss it. Those who seek, find. To those who knock, it is opened."

But with all this said, Lewis still recognized the ultimate futility of all his speculation when he wrote in *Letters to Malcom*: "Guesses, of course, only guesses. If they are not true, something better will be."

Writing *Malcom* late in life, Lewis appears to have traveled past his need for intellectual certainty and arrived at a place we all need to visit: the simple trust that God always has something better for us than we could ever imagine for ourselves, that his love is the sufficient stuff that casts out all fear if we will allow.

In the face of all we can't know herenow, we can always choose to start with what we do know. The message Yeshua poured out his life delivering, the message that Scripture mirrors once we put its words back into their original context, is that God is Unity—complete identification with all that is and lives and breathes—which looks like what we call love, which means that God is also love, a love that is free and unconditional because it isn't performed, it just exists as itself, as pure connection.

Starting there, like the ancient Hebrews who viewed the afterlife not as proven fact, but more of an essential extension of God's justice—that is, any wrongs not righted in this life must be righted in the next (so there must be one)—maybe we can view the existence of hell in the same way. If Yeshua's good news of unconditional love is as real as justice, then God will never turn his back on anyone, ever—will always be drawing everyone toward himself, toward Unity, forever. And hell's existence and nature must somehow extend the reality of *love's* existence and nature.

If we begin to conceive of hell as an extension of love rather than an extension of fear—that is, any unity not realized in this life must somehow be realized in the next—we begin the process of granting ourselves permission to believe that hell's inhabitants are not put there by God or kept there by God, but even as they suffer the flames of their own separation, they are always in the presence of the possibility of a different reality.

No one can confirm or deny, prove or disprove such a statement; I make it only out of the deep conviction that God really is love—that no matter how far we stray from the Way, God will always leave a trail of breadcrumbs, a Way back to shelter under his wings, if we are only willing. But regardless of whatever any of us can prove to one another, until we have proven to ourselves that God is love and that love is forever and free, we will always live with fear as our default position.

Someone once wrote to me in response to some of this:

"Good grief, you can't have the Good News without the bad news." But it seems to me...

The Good News is: *there is no bad news.*

If Yeshua is right, we're as forgiven as we want to be. We're as saved as we want to be. In God's heart, we've always been forgiven. In God's heart, we've always been saved.

Anticipating the next obvious question, Paul asks at Romans 6, "What then will we say? Shall we continue in sin that grace may abound?" And Paul answers himself: may it never be. How can those who have died to separation and disunity continue to live there? Perfectly stated. As we gain more direct experience of God; we can stop seeing him merely as police, judge, and jailer, and begin to realize that though God is exactly the consummate lover that Yeshua models, it is always our choice whether to enter into the acceptance that is freely offered.

Which means if we're ever to experience the love that casts out fear, we still need to *repent*—understood Hebraically not as remorse or regret, but as an affirmative change of direction, a move God-ward, away from behavior that separates and toward the acceptance that always beckons. And in the flow of that love we may begin to understand judgment no longer in terms of God's decision about us, about where we spend eternity, but as *our decision* about God: whether we've become people able to see and accept God as God really is.

Maybe hell is not a place, but a person unprepared to recognize God as God, walking right past him on the endless way to the god he or she expects to see.

Where is our fear if there is no power hell or any of its inhabitants have over us that we don't give it or them? Fearing hell only puts us in hell *herenow* by denying a love that would never do so *therethen*.

Or as John says in his Gospel at chapter 3, "For God did not send his son into the world to condemn the world, but to save (liberate, forgive, heal, deliver) the world through him. Whoever believes (trusts) in him is not condemned, but whoever does not believe (trust) stands condemned already..." It seems hell is not a judgment or a sentence, but an immediate choice—and we hold the lever.

Whatever hell really is will be revealed in time. It's not for us to know such things right now. But Yeshua is saying we know enough to let hell be—that thinking about it only keeps us in its suburbs every moment of our lives.

Time to move to the country, get some fresh air.

CHALLENGE
Fear of the Lord never includes being afraid of the Lord;
fear of punishment never matures into trust in love.

TRADITION
The goal of spiritual practice is clarity;
the more we understand, the more we trust.

Freefall

TRUST

Before you jump, you can know
everything and nothing at the same time.

I HAD ASSUMPTIONS ABOUT SKYDIVING. ALMOST NONE OF THEM
turned out to be true. I had assumptions about marriage and
parenthood too...

Before you jump, it's easy to think you know all about the big
things in life. You watch people do them; they become familiar. You
see them on TV, in the movies, in the news; they become common-
place. People around you are constantly doing the things they do
until you think you know all about them.

Before you jump, it's easy to think that the table of contents, the
dictionary definition, the executive summary of a thing accurately
represents the thing itself. Like the Cliff's Notes you read in school
to get a grade instead of the book that was written to express a life,
it's easy to forget you can know all about a thing without knowing
anything of it. You may think you know about things like *Moby Dick*
and marriage, but until you've been lashed to the whale of your
obsessions alongside Ahab or perched on a pile of anniversaries high
enough to see the broad contours of your family's life, your theories
remain untested; your assumptions invalid.

Skydiving is like this, like the big things in life. Maybe it has to do with the falling—like falling in love or taking a fall or falling down drunk, there is a laying aside, a laying open, an intensity and abandon, a point of no return that can't be communicated in anything but the first person.

Before you jump, you can know everything and nothing at the same time.

☉ ⨀ ⨁ ⨁ ⨍

I arrived at the Perris Valley Skydiving Center early in the morning. There were many of us. We all crunched through the dirt and gravel of the parking lot in cars of every make and color; people of every make and color covertly watching each other flow toward the pair of single-wide mobile homes serving as offices for the Center. Herded inside, we were seated in front of a large TV monitor, welcomed in cheerful tones, and told to watch the screen. A fifteen-minute presentation detailed everything that could possibly go wrong with a jump: landing in water, landing in power lines, chute failures, and the worst nightmare: getting tangled in the lines of your own chute so you couldn't cut it away and pull the reserve. Feet were shuffling through this, some sideways glances to check a friend's reaction.

At the end of the presentation, a lawyer for the Center appeared on the screen seated at his desk in a suit telling us how we needed to perfectly understand the risks we were about to take: how we were doing this of our own free will, taking full responsibility for all the things that could happen to us—death, dismemberment, paralysis—and how we would be legally holding the Center harmless for any such unfortunate circumstances aforementioned. He described the legal waiver of liability that we would be signing as a live staff member passed them out, telling us to read carefully. Another staff member brought out a video camera on a tripod and aimed it at us, telling us to stand and read the terms of the waiver out loud, while the little red light recorded against such time as any of us or our heirs should decide to disagree. We read, we signed, we walked back out onto the dirt a bit quieter than we went in.

I had signed up for an accelerated freefall, or AFF as it appeared in the brochure, which meant I would not be strapped to a jump-master, but would fall with two jumpmasters on either side holding my legstraps until I pulled the cord and was on my own for the rest of the jump. An AFF required a full eight hours of training on the ground before making the jump at the end of the day, so I and the other AFFers made our way to a permanent building near the mobile homes to find our classroom.

Our instructor must never have gotten tired of watching each first-timer walk into his classroom and register the look of shock none of us could conceal as we realized he only had one leg. He wasn't the least bit shy about it. This was no human-like prosthesis trying to look like a limb—his left pant leg was cut off at mid-thigh to fully expose a spring-loaded shock absorber, a metal and rubber pogo stick attached to his stump. All he needed was a parrot and an eye-patch.

He savored the moment until we were all seated around him. "The first thing I want you to know is that I didn't lose my leg skydiving." The laughter came out a bit too fast and high-pitched, but no one left, so we began. Throughout the day, we learned all about jumping out of planes over two miles off the ground and the gear that would let us live to tell about it. We learned about the aerodynamics of a falling leaf and how to mimic that, spread-eagled with our backs arched; about terminal velocity, that we would not be falling any faster than around 120 miles per hour—not much comfort there. We learned about the gear, the parachutes and how they were packed, about the reserve chutes and how they were packed by a certified packer who put his or her lead seal on each pack, and about how they would lose their reputation and certification if their chute failed and we died. "Their reputation, your life," was I think how pegleg put it.

We learned about altimeters and the circle of awareness that would take us though freefall and prepare us to safely open our chutes. We learned about what to do if something went wrong: if we landed in water or in power lines or trees, if our main chute was damaged or tangled, or if we got tangled in our own lines. (Mostly we just learned not to let that happen.) We learned about how we were going to time our jump with our jumpmasters—one, two, three, jump—and how to fly ourselves in for a landing: how to work the toggles to turn and brake, find the landing strip, the windsock, make our first pass with the wind and our final pass against it; to "flare" just before landing, bringing both toggles down at the same time to brake and step gracefully back on the ground. We learned all about skydiving, got all the information we needed, thoroughly and professionally delivered. The only thing left was to go and be fitted for our gear, so we filed back out onto the dirt and into a big barn of a room lined with jumpsuits and helmets and goggles and packs.

And all day long I was feeling it in my stomach and chest. From the lawyer in the suit to the instructor on the peg to the images of disaster to the approaching reality of an open door and a lot of air, it grew stronger down there, filling me with questions of whether I was really going through with this, whether I would really get on board the plane, really let go and just fall. It sat on my chest as I found a jumpsuit that fit, a helmet, goggles—as pegleg helped me into a pack like a gentleman with a lady's coat, except for the legstraps part. It followed me out to the airstrip, waited with me as I watched the *King Air* land empty, its passengers all having abandoned it, and climbed with me into the bare fuselage.

There were so many of us inside—each jumper with two jumpmasters and some with a videographer as well—we sat spread-legged on the curved and seamed bottom of a metal tube, inside the legs of the person behind with the pack of the person in front pressed against our chests. There was no door, just an opening in the side of the fuselage as the engines whined up to speed. For the first time that day, there was nothing to do but sit and wait as we taxied, as we lifted off and climbed to our target altitude, as cold metal seeped through the backside of jumpsuits and orange afternoon sun in the shape of small windows played across our little space when the *King Air* banked into position.

I looked down over the two rows of helmets in front of me wondering what was going on inside each of them when suddenly I thought of D-Day, of how I'd learned about the paratroopers as a kid, reading and rereading all the stories I could find about their nighttime jump behind enemy lines before the beach assault began. I thought about the rows of helmets in those dark planes and with my new insight, wondered what they had been feeling as they prepared to jump. Not into the warm sunlight of inland California, but the pitch-blackness of wartime France; not into the waiting arms of their jumpmasters with everything in the air and on the ground designed for safety, but into the guns and knives of the Nazis, with everything in the air and on the ground designed to kill. Anything I was feeling, anything I was experiencing, could only remind me of the impossibility of ever really knowing what those boys felt as their planes climbed into position in the dark. Before I jumped, I had the luxury of ignorance, of believing my reading and study had really taken me there. Before I jumped, I thought I knew. Now I knew more—and less at the same time.

I heard my name and it was time. I struggled to my feet and picked my way over legs and riveted metal seams to the opening with all that air behind it. I stood in the wind holding on to the edges waiting for my jumpmasters to get into position. From 12,500 feet, the ground looked like a painting, not real at all; it looked as flat and dimensionless as any movie or TV image, but my lunch was at the base of my throat—that was different as I got the signal to count: one, two...but suddenly I couldn't remember if we jumped on three or after three, and as I pushed off I realized I was alone.

And there was this incredible rush of air but I couldn't breathe it, couldn't exhale enough to get any more in. I'd really done it, I'd set in motion a sequence of events that would end on the ground one way or another—either in a graceful step under a bright canopy or at 120 miles an hour. I'd done it, and there was no way to take it back. There was only me and two miles of air and a nylon bedsheet on my back that would make all the difference.

Suddenly my jumpmasters were back with me, both their faces lowering into view on either side. They shouted instructions in my ears as we went through the circle of awareness and checked the big altimeter strapped on my chest. We were ready; we'd done all we could do until the dial read five thousand and it was time to pull.

They told me to enjoy the ride.

Falling together in perfect unison isn't like falling at all. I assumed freefall would be like a roller coaster, the heart-in-throat squeeze into the back of my seat all the way down, but it was like that only for those first few breathless seconds of acceleration. As I opened into the falling leaf shape and gravity and air pressure stabilized, I could have been sitting in a living room with my two new friends over tea; there was no sense of motion at all—except for the 120-mile-an-hour wind in my face. It was more like flying, like hovering, like the giddy freedom of all those air dreams. I could see the whole Perris Valley from end to end, the string of mountains beneath the lowering sun, the flat valley floor, lined and patched, directly below. It seemed static, frozen, as if we hovered above, until I noticed that objects on the ground were slowly getting larger—slowly, like the hands on a clock. It seemed so slight, so benign, but sobering too.

Then there was shouting in my ears. I looked at the altimeter and it was already at five thousand, but I blinked at it for another second or two as the shouting continued realizing that I had been so completely immersed in the ride that I had forgotten about the passage of time or altitude. I had forgotten about the circle of awareness and the meter on my chest. I had even forgotten to be afraid.

All day long I had been afraid, even though all day long I'd had a choice. I could have said no to the lawyer or the one-legged instructor. I could have walked back to my car from the fitting barn or from the steps of the *King Air*. Even as long as I was clinging to the edge of that hole in the fuselage, I still had a choice to go or not, and as long as I had a choice, I also had fear. In a way I hadn't assumed, it was the choice itself that created and maintained the fear I felt. What if I made the wrong choice? What if my choice led to disaster? Or shame and regret? At the beginning of the day, I'd had many choices, but all day long through the hours of training and preparation, those choices had been falling away, one by one, with the passage of time and the path taken until I stood at the edge with only one choice left: to simply let go and let fall, or not.

And with just the relaxing of my fingers, even that last choice fell away leaving nothing left to cling to in an ocean of rushing air. There was no awareness of time or concern or even my own thoughts—nothing left but the ride and a meter reading five thousand feet. I pulled the cord, felt the violent tug at my legstraps as the two faces at my left and right shot straight down out of sight. Alone again, I looked up as I was trained to do, and my canopy was big and orange and perfectly filled with air. Everything had gone suddenly silent. There seemed not to be a breath of wind as, instead of falling through it, I was being gently ushered along with it. I reached up to grab the toggles and ride my sail home.

Before I jumped, I could never have imagined the impact of hanging from slender white threads and watching the tops of my boots suspended above a mile of nothing but silent space. Before I jumped, I would never have assumed my boots would be my most lasting image, the one I can still see through closed eyes from a distance of over fifteen years. Before I jumped, I could never have told you about the feeling of total release and liberation—forgiveness, even—from a day of constant fear.

As long as I had one last thing to cling to, I had a choice. As long as I had one last thing to cling to, I was afraid. As long as I had a choice, a decision to make, I could fail. But with the letting go, with the last thing left to hold on to receding into a deep sky, there was nothing left to do but what I already knew how to do, what I was trained to do—and to enjoy the ride. As soon as I let go and left all my choices behind, I wasn't afraid anymore.

Before I jumped, I couldn't have told you any of this, and before you jump, you'll never really know what I mean.

○ ⊘ ⊕ ⊕ ⊗

We're all skydivers. We're all skydiving.

Right now, this moment, we're freefalling. I'm falling, you're falling, and since we're all falling together in unison, we're not aware; there's no sense of motion. But if we stop and really focus on the objects around us, we can see them slowly growing larger and marking our passage. From the moment of birth, from the moment we were pushed out of our mother's fuselage, we've been falling ever since—a series of events set in motion that will end at the moment of our death, no matter what we do or how we feel about it. The commitment was made without our permission, the point of no return crossed. One way or another, the ground of our death is coming up to meet us and the only choice we have is how to meet it back: in a graceful step under a bright canopy or kicking and screaming at 120 miles an hour.

But if only it were that easy. To stretch it further, it's as if we've been pushed out of our plane in the blackness of night from an unknown altitude with no altimeter—we don't know the height from which we started and can't see the ground at which we'll stop. How long will we fall? Sixty or seventy years? Thirty years? Until the end of the day? It's the unknowing that does it to us. It's the unknowing that makes informed choices impossible and the search for clarity a cruel joke. It's the unknowing that scares us. It scares us so much that most of us choose to live without making a choice, choose to live as if still standing at the open door, trembling under the weight of all those unmade choices.

But we're already out the door and falling—have been falling for as long as we've been alive. Continuing to live as if we're still clinging to the door of our plane is illusion, self-deception. We're living the anxiety, tension, and fear of trying to make a choice that has long been made, in the doorway of a plane that is long gone, landed and in the hanger, the pilot home having dinner.

The mind is a powerful thing:
the reality we believe is the reality we endure.

If we believe our choice is yet unmade and that we're still standing at the door, then we will experience our lives as if frozen there: waiting, wondering, searching, clinging, fearing everything and enjoying nothing right until the moment we rush headlong into the ground we didn't see coming. Ready or not, the ground doesn't care what we believe; it's out there in the dark, coming at us at 120 miles an hour. We can't enjoy the ride until we realize that we're already freefalling, have always been, that the choice to jump was never ours to make. Accepting the fact of our falling, making friends with that central fact of life comes well before we can ever learn to like it. How do you fight freefall anyway? By pretending there's one last thing in our grasp to cling to? By praying it away?

123

And what is the most common prayer we pray? "Lord, please put me back in the airplane..." Of course it's not voiced that way, but that's exactly what we mean when we feel ourselves falling and ask God to change our circumstances, to stop the ride, to undo what's been done to us, to undo what we've done to ourselves or to do what we've left undone. Yeshua sweating blood in the Garden of Gethsemane: "Father, if it's possible, take this cup away from me..." Stop the world, I want to get off. If you thought Yeshua was immune to the pain and fear we all feel, think again, but moving through it, he reconnects with his Father's deepest purpose and pushes off, "...not my will, but yours..." freely falling again. Paul praying for years for God to remove the thorn in his side, to take away the pain, the irritation, the frustration of whatever it was that kept him awake at night and dampened his dreams. But then at the end of his life awaiting execution in a Roman prison, he pens some of the most beautiful and hopeful verses in all of Scripture. Pushed off, a graceful falling leaf.

The second most common prayer? "Lord, if you won't put me back in the plane, at least show me the ground." We call this a prayer for clarity, wisdom, or discernment; it sounds noble and looks good on paper, but all we really want is someone to tell us exactly what to do, to figure it all out, remove all the unknowns and risk before we make the first move to relax our grip.

Brennan Manning tells a wonderful story in his book, *Ruthless Trust*:

> When the brilliant ethicist John Kavanaugh went to work for three months at "the house of the dying" in Calcutta, he was seeking a clear answer as to how best to spend the rest of his life. On the first morning there he met Mother Teresa. She asked, "And what can I do for you?" Kavanaugh asked her to pray for him.

"What do you want me to pray for?" she asked. He voiced the request that he had borne thousands of miles from the United States, "Pray that I have clarity."

She said firmly, "No, I will not do that." When he asked her why, she said, "Clarity is the last thing you are clinging to and must let go of." When Kavanaugh commented that she always seemed to have the clarity he longed for, she laughed and said, "I have never had clarity; what I have always had is trust. So I will pray that you trust God."

What is the last thing you are clinging to?

Whatever it is, however noble or important it may seem, it is the last thing keeping you imprisoned, keeping you from flight. It is the last thing keeping you afraid and the first thing you must let go of.

At one time or another, we all think clarity is the answer, but it's just the edge of another door in the sky, something to cling to, a reason to procrastinate, to forestall what we already know how to do. We cling to clarity as the only means by which we can make the right choice—as if there's only one choice that is right, that will take us to the right destination—as if there's only one destination that is right. We keep all our choices safe in the pockets of our jumpsuits, waiting on the clarity that will remove the risk of letting go and letting fall. But clarity never comes in the way we expect and risk is never removed; there is only the moment that we choose to act as if there is clarity, as if there is no risk—to trust our training and our gear and the people telling us we can survive all this. Or not.

As important as our choices may be, it's *making* a choice that is essential, and any choice is better than trembling at the door of the *King Air*. What is the last thing you are clinging to? It's the very thing keeping you fearful, afraid to fall away and begin enjoying the ride.

Looking from the outside in, the person who trusts looks serene. The person who trusts always seems to have the clarity we long for, the assurance of their choices, the facts at their disposal, the unfair advantage of a peek behind the curtain. But trust doesn't work from the outside in any more than Kingdom, and from the inside out, from his or her point of view, the person who trusts has no more clarity than we've got—no more facts or figures or assurances, no better view of distant objects or the immediate future. They make their choices just as we do, weighing whatever risk is present and whatever partial information is available against their passions and desires and whatever seems best.

The difference is that they know they are already falling and not clinging to the door of the plane; that no choice they make can change their ultimate trajectory, only the quality of their fall; and somehow they know their sail will open, big and orange above them, and that they'll be stepping gracefully to the ground at the end of their ride. With the big choice already made, little choices can be negotiated with lightness and a smile and the enjoyment that attracts brilliant ethicists halfway around the world to the door of a tiny woman living in the worst part of Calcutta.

◐ ◑ ⊕ ⊕ ⊘

Trust has nothing to do with clarity; those with the least clarity, the children and children-at-heart among us, have the most trust. Richard Foster writes in his foreword to *Ruthless Trust,*

> When our children were young I would sometimes rise early on a Saturday morning and fix them pancakes for breakfast. It was all great fun—the broken eggs, the spilt milk, the batter and the chatter. They loved pancakes—even my pancakes—and they would wolf them down quickly. I would often watch in astonishment at their greedy eating. Not once did I see either of them

slipping a few pancakes under the table, stuffing them in their pockets thinking, "I don't know about Dad. Maybe there won't be any pancakes tomorrow and so I'd better get myself a little stash just in case." Not once did they ask me about the price of eggs or my ability to secure enough milk for tomorrow. No, as far as they were concerned there was an endless supply of pancakes. They lived, you see, in trust.

Trust has nothing to do with effort either; trust is the effortless result of the experience of trustworthiness. My daughter would often ask me for my car keys while I was working at the church, wanting to get something out of the car or just as an excuse to go exploring. Not being born yesterday, I knew what happened to keys in the hands of eight or nine-year-olds, so I'd always say no, and walk with her out to the parking lot. After one too many interruptions, I thought for a second, pulled her over and gave her the long lecture about keys and responsibility, after which she still had to pull them from between my fingers leaving me to watch her and my keys move out of sight as if for the last time. But the keys came right back, so next time, she got the keys with a mini-lecture, then with just a stern, reminder-look, and eventually, she'd just shout at me, "Dad, keys," and I'd toss them across the room in mid-stride.

No amount of effort on earth could make me trust my daughter, but once I experienced her trustworthiness, no amount of effort was needed. I just had to have enough faith in her to take the first step, the initial risk. I had to push off from my fears and fall with her for a while before I could relax and begin to enjoy the ride. "Without faith, it is impossible to please God," but when we forget that faith in Scripture is never separated from trust, we make the mistake of thinking that faith—acting in spite of risk and doubt—is the goal, the end product. Faith is only the means to the end of trust, of falling with God to experience his trustworthiness.

"Faith without works is dead," but we make the mistake of thinking that the works of faith are the good deeds we do that prove our faith. That's much too close to *earning* our faith, much too close to legalism, and much too far from the truth that makes us free. The work of faith, the proof that faith is alive and kicking, is trust. Effortless trust. Smiling trust. Trust with a smooth brow and a steady gaze.

The work of faith is not what we do through our own effort, but what comes effortlessly to us as we move out in spite of the risks. When we effortlessly find ourselves tossing our keys to God, casually releasing the last thing we are clinging to, our faith has graduated to trust, and we are freely falling.

And the choice made, the falling acknowledged, what then? What do we feel, experience, know? Is there a sudden rush of clarity and insight filling us at 120 miles an hour? A constant euphoria and sense of peace? The removal of all our problem circumstances?

At Kings 19, Elijah is in despair, fearing for his life and hiding in a cave unable to make his next move. He hears a great wind tearing into the mountain, but the Lord is not in the wind. There is an earthquake, then a fire, but he knows the Lord is not in these great signs either. It's when he hears a soft blowing, a breath at the back of his awareness, that he wraps his face in his mantle and goes out to fall with God.

We all have assumptions about trust.

From the outside in, from the airplane or the ground, trust looks huge and spectacular—like courage or clarity, faith or piety, knowledge or even foreknowledge—so we assume it is. But from the inside out, from inside that helmet looking out through those scratched and worn goggles, it's a very slight thing, easy to overlook, even easier to dismiss. It changes nothing and everything: nothing of circumstance or risk, but everything of our ability to move out, off, through, and over. It is the tiniest stirring that allows us to act in spite of all our fears, to start rolling, like a snowball, gathering more assurance the longer we fall.

Once more from Brennan Manning:

> Ruthless trust is an unerring sense, way deep down, that beneath the surface agitation, boredom, and insecurity of life, it's gonna be all right. Ill winds may blow, more character defects may surface, sickness may visit, and friends will surely die; but a stubborn, irrefutable certainty persists that God is with us and loves us in our struggle to be faithful. A nonrational, absolutely true intuition perdures that there is something unfathomably big in the universe, something that points to Someone who is filled with peace and power, love and undreamed of creativity—Someone who inevitably will reconcile all things in himself... Thus it may mean more to Jesus when we say, "I trust you," than when we say, "I love you."

How much easier is it to say, "I love you" than "I trust you?" We say we love all the time, but what does it cost? What does it mean? How do we prove it? What are the risks? But to say I trust you, means we have an experience, a history; we have risked something, put ourselves on the line. It means we have the scars and the x-rays to show for our time in the field of our lives. "I love you" can be said at any time, for any reason, but "I trust you" only comes after falling together, knowing together.

When we fall with God, we leave our assumptions behind and begin to know, to *yida*, his complete trustworthiness. We don't get all the answers or clarity or removal of risk, but we do get enough of a sense of security to take the next step—and the next. Trust doesn't change the circumstances of our lives, but it changes the perception of those circumstances. It puts them into a perspective that allows us to begin to enjoy ourselves however difficult they may be.

"I have learned to be content in whatever circumstances I am." Writing from his prison cell, Paul is saying to the Philippians and to us that he had learned to make friends with life—not to keep trying to wish or pray it into a shape of his liking, but to begin to like the shape it had. It didn't happen overnight; life is often not likable enough that we would ever want to be its friend. But it happened for Paul as he continued to fall: at some point he reached out, introduced himself and shook hands with life, accepted it on its own terms, and began to enjoy the ride.

What's the last thing you're holding on to and need to let go of? Clarity? Wisdom? Knowledge? Faith? Power? Money? Talent?

Relax your grip. Let it go. Push off. Fall away.

☾ ◑ ⊕ ⊕ ⊗

Can you remember being ten years old during the long, hot summers that seemed to go on forever between the books and clocks of school and before big boy or girl pressures set in? Go there. Right now. Be ten years old again, in your swimsuit, the afternoon sun hot on your skin as you run around your friend's swimming pool. Add your shouts and squeals to all those around you, add your energy and motion to the chaotic scene. Can you see it? The brilliant sunlight shimmering off the water, the colorful swimsuits and brown skin, the constant motion and water slopping over the sides? It's all there as you drink it in, watching the scene and becoming part of it as you run to the edge of the pool turning to face away, your back to the water. Wet toes curling around the concrete lip turn white as you grip there, heels out over the water. You hold your arms out straight from shoulder height, sparkling drops clinging as you tilt your head back and close your eyes.

Last time you looked, the pool was filled with shimmering blue water. Last time you looked, your friends all bobbed around the edges watching you with expectant smiles. You believe the water is still there, that the scene remains exactly as it did the last time you looked, and that the water will catch you and shock you and thrill you when you fall back into it. The last time you looked, you believed all this—you believe it now. But you won't know that your belief has turned to faith until you push down with your toes, feel your center of gravity shift backwards in that dizzy tilt, and know that the line has been crossed, and there's no turning back.

And you fall. Slowly at first, gaining speed through those heart-stopping moments as you wait for it to come—the cold, hard slap against your back, the sinking down into coolness, springing back up from the bottom to break the surface into sunshine and laughter as you shake your head, wipe your eyes, and scan the ring of faces around you.

There is a breath, a moment filled with wide eyes and dripping noses. It's the moment you finally know, but won't recognize for some time, that your faith has graduated to trust. It's the moment you break for the sides and yell to your friends over your shoulder,

"Let's do it again!"

CHALLENGE
*Mental effort has nothing to do with trust;
repeated experience alone creates the sense of risk-free-ness we call trust.*

TRADITION
*Church, prayer, and worship create sacred space,
places we can go to meet God.*

Stars Beneath Our Feet

PRESENCE

See, I am with you always even to the end of the age.

Matthew 28:20

Road trip.

DEATH VALLEY IN FEBRUARY. ONE OF THE HOTTEST AND DRIEST spots in the world, but arriving late at night, around eleven at the tail end of winter, temperatures were only in the high seventies with no moon and a dark sky. A large dune field lay just a few miles outside the little town, and I really wanted to see the stars. Though no one lobbies or fights to protect them as they do tigers and rare tadpoles, stars are an endangered species too—at least in the city. So I drove out to the dunes and then walked out several hundred yards, sliding on the slip faces and watching for anything poisonous in the small circle the flashlight threw on the sand. I walked until the world was nothing but dunes and sky and the faint outline of ragged, black mountains circling at a respectful distance. Sat down, turned out my light, and looked up.

Cold sand, fine like talcum. Warm air. Waiting for eyes to adjust...

In the city, it's hard to remember what the night sky really looks like. What it's supposed to look like. What it looked like every night to our ancestors before the lights on the ground pushed back against the lights in the sky and prevailed—partial constellations limping westward like multiple amputees. It's good to be reminded. To sit under a sky that you forgot existed, that takes your breath away with sheer magnitude and number. To see the hazy band of the plane of the galaxy itself angling through a star field so dense that you can only feel inconsequential in response. Watching the whole living sheet turning: all those specks above burning down on all the specks beneath—a few actually burning back. Like me, that night. Making my pilgrimage deep into the Mojave to find the stars.

And there, on my dune of choice, feeling closer to them—why? Because I could see them? I suppose so. But stars are all around me right now. I don't have to wait for nightfall or go somewhere remote with really dark sky to be in their presence. They didn't go anywhere at sunrise this morning—they were still there burning away right where they were before the nearby star climbed into view scattering its light though the air and turning black to gold and gold to light blue. Curtain down.

The stars are still right there, and not just above my head. There are stars beneath my feet. It's just that this ball I'm standing on is in the way. Remove the ball, float freely in space and see stars in every possible direction, equal density and distribution. There is no up or down or right or left, forward or back. Just stars—everywhere I look—disorienting, disturbing. What is it I really stand on if there are stars beneath my feet?

And now the most brilliant of our thinkers and scientists tell us that this is the way it always looks from wherever we look in the universe. That the universe is finite, but has no edge—that even though it is not forever in expanse and is not all there is, if we start out in any direction, no matter how long we travel, we will never get to the end or edge of it. We will never see a view any different than the one we see right here; the stars will never thin out in front of us and disappear so we can look back at the ball of the universe.

From any direction we start out, we will always end up back where we started again, like traveling the surface inside a ping pong ball, a single black hole where everything has closed in on itself, sealed over in curved space. In the most real way, every point in the universe is exactly at the center of the universe because any other position is meaningless. From wherever we are looking, the view is always the same because we are always at the center of all things; there is nowhere else to be, because we are always there, in the center, wherever we are.

It's fascinating that theoretical science is just now catching on to what we should have always known spiritually. That in the utmost details of things, matter and energy, body and spirit do follow the same path. Our journey of spirit also has no edge. We will never get to the end of it, and we are always at the center of it. There is no up, down, right left, forward, back, no sense of direction at all. Or passage of time. The view is always the same as we always remain in the center of God. God is like that, always keeping each of us in the center of all his things.

And God is always right here and right now, perhaps obscured by the bright burning of the nearby star of our own consciousness, but if we learn to set our conscious thoughtstream down for a time like the setting of the sun into night, we will find him right here, right where we left him, visible again, burning brightly with us at the center of all his things. In every direction we look. Equal density and distribution. Always.

I left the desert the next day.
I couldn't see them, but stars came with me.

☽ ☽ ☽ ⊕ ⊕

I love when science finally catches up with Scripture. Or less condescendingly, I love when we finally realize that ultimately, science and Scripture will agree. And why shouldn't they? The things of God that have been revealed to us were written into the physical fabric of the universe long before they were written on our hearts or in our books. It is the intuitive nature of Scripture to arrive first, in a straight shot, with the analytical nature of science slowly circling in, step by step, but bringing much greater physical credibility as it arrives.

I remember reading about the tunnel of Samos—a four thousand foot aqueduct cut right through the heart of a mountain 2,600 years ago in ancient Greece. The tunnel is considered an ancient wonder because two teams cut through the limestone from opposite sides of the mountain, meeting in the middle with their ceilings only four centimeters offset after digging almost a half a mile each. Using only picks and shovels without magnetic compasses or modern surveying instruments, no one is really sure how they did it, hacking away in the dark with only their calculations to guide them until they broke in on each other in the center of a mountain.

Science and Scripture are like this: two teams digging into the mountain of God's truth from opposite sides—one from an empirical, mathematical, or theoretical examination of the evidence of the universe and the other from a direct, mystical revelation from the Maker of the universe himself. As they labor away in the dark, each side often has only contemptuous and completely dismissive things to say about the other, but when calculations and revelations are sure, imagine their surprise to break in on each other in the center of all God's things. And yet, it had to be so: there's only one truth at the center, so no matter how we journey or from what premise we begin, if our journey is true, destination is identical, unified. If not, then one side or the other has lost its Way.

If God loves us in such a way that we are all his favorites, all securely held in the center of his heart, why wouldn't that truth be written into a universe in which we are all physically located in the very center as well? That the best theoretical minds we have produced, the ones taking the longest peeks behind the curtain, are also becoming convinced that this is so, is a breaking through from the side of science into territory long occupied by Scripture in the heart of God's mountain.

In the very last verse of the very last chapter of Matthew, Yeshua tells us he will always be with us, even to the end of the age. But this promise of his presence doesn't come unaccompanied: he and the Father are one—always present to each other, so it's a package deal. As when Moses asks Yahweh God who it is that is addressing him from the burning bush, the same promise of unending presence is the response. *Hayah asher hayah*, "I am that I am" is another way of saying, "I am with you always at the center of all things," that Presence itself is the ultimate reality.

But what does this promise of constant presence really mean? How does it help direct our journey to the center of God's mountain when our awareness, our experience of God's presence is anything but constant? The Scriptures themselves are full of references to God turning his back on us, refusing to answer us, forgetting us... Yeshua quotes David's Psalm 22 from the cross in asking the age-old question, "My God, my God, why have you forsaken me?"

If we don't recognize that David's psalm and Hebrew scripture in general unapologetically oscillate between the realities of human experience and the realities of God's nature, Scripture will confuse the two in our minds, making God's nature look more like our own. And as long as we don't really understand presence, God's promise of his presence can quickly become abstract, academic, a dry item in a creed to be memorized but not experienced with any reliability. If we don't see him or feel him, if our problems in life remain unchanged, if a tree falls in the forest with no one there to hear it, is there really any sound, any presence at all?

We need a better way to understand the nature of presence.

○ ◑ ⊕ ⊕ ⊘

If I'm here, I'm not anywhere else.

What at first seems self-evident, a truism, with a closer look, makes a huge statement about the value of our presence. We are finite creatures—we are only physically present here for a limited amount of time, and we can only be present one place at a time. This "tyranny of the finite" forces us to make choices about where we place our presence. To say yes to anything is to say no to something else. We can't be everywhere at once, and we don't have the unlimited time to be everywhere eventually. Finiteness gives value to life: we value everything based on its availability; the less there is of a thing, the more we value it, and vice versa. Supply and demand.

Spend some time with anyone overly focused either on reincarnation or an everlasting afterlife and see how the value of this fleeting life herenow is diminished in direct proportion to the availability of recurring earthly lives or an unlimited heavenly one. We value our lives because they are short; we see our choices in life as important because they define the quality of that short span of our presence.

Our lives here are defined by our time here. Our time here is defined by our presence. And where we choose to place our presence defines the quality and experience of our lives. In other words, we spend the time of our lives by choosing where to place our presence. Our presence is really all we have to work with, the only thing that is really ours to give, and ultimately, our lives are judged in the eyes of others by the succession of places at which we've chosen to be present. Our choice of where we place this most valuable thing, the only thing we really possess, says everything about us as persons.

If I'm here, I'm not anywhere else. If I'm here, it's because I made a conscious choice to be here and nowhere else. Out of all the possible places I could have been, I chose this place, this time, as the most important place I could be. What a statement that makes to everyone around me...the greatest gift I can ever give to another is the gift of my presence. With my presence, I am actually giving the very stuff of which my life is made—I'm giving my life away, laying down my life for my friends. Yeshua said there is no greater gift than this, no greater love. The gift of our presence is the ultimate expression of love: "I love you enough that being here with you is my highest priority—I said no to everything and everyone else in the world to be with you right here, right now."

My finiteness makes such a statement possible.

Think about the most significant moments in life. A wedding, a funeral, the birth of a child, a birthday, a hospital stay, a graduation or a first day of school, Christmas, Thanksgiving, a bon voyage or a homecoming, a baptism or bar mitzvah or ordination, a new job, a layoff, or maybe just a lonely moment when you really need a knock at the door. What does it mean to have someone's presence at a moment like one of these? How much would these moments be diminished if those you loved most were not present to share them with you?

As president of a non-profit organization, I recently attended the funeral of one of our donors. I'd just been getting to know him personally and had only met him once, but I had felt an immediate connection with him and then sharply the sudden loss of his presence—even if only across a phone line or email reader. Still, I was unprepared for how much it seemed to mean to his widow to have my presence at the service. She took my hand in both of hers and thanked me with brimming eyes—sent a letter afterward thanking me again. I had never met her or spoken to her before, and had almost decided not to go up and speak to her at all, thinking I'd just be in the way, a distraction—that the presence of someone she didn't even know would bring no value or comfort to her.

For someone to say that your wedding, your birthday, your moment is the most important thing in the world right now, is immense, incalculable in value. And this is exactly what we are saying to each other with the simple fact of our presence.

If you throw a party, the presence of your invited guests is what you crave. Yeshua told several parables of kings and landowners inviting guests to wedding feasts, and of their reactions when the invited guests didn't choose to be present. You judge the success of your party (and by extension yourself) by the number and quality of people who were present. "How many people came?" "Who was there?" You often judge whether you want to be present at someone else's party, or any event, based on whom else may be present, "Who's going to be there?"

Certain people actually impart importance or legitimacy to a gathering simply through their presence, and those people are actively sought out to elevate the status of the gathering. What if the President of the United States decided to come to your birthday party? Suddenly, no matter who you are, your little party is transformed into global breaking news. In our culture, celebrities are always in demand to bring attention and attendance to events, and are even paid for the favor of their presence—which begs another question, the question of motive.

If I'm here, do I really want to be here?

Every one of us has experienced having a conversation with someone who was obviously only waiting to speak rather than really listening, looking around the room for the person with whom they'd rather be speaking, checking a watch, or taking each and every cell phone call received and maybe even making a few. Even though he or she is here, he or she is not present. In trying to be two places at once, they are nowhere at all.

Writing at the computer just now, my two-year-old son comes running up babbling something about jellyfish as if his life depended on it. My instinct is to try to retain whatever shreds of my last thought are still reachable and without taking my eyes off the screen, say just enough to send him trotting off still smiling and babbling. Here with him, but not present, there is no exchange or connection. No gift. I'd like to say that I now always do, but can only say I mostly do, push away from the computer and pull him into my lap or take his face in my hands and look in those impossibly big eyes as he reels off whatever is so important to him and so incomprehensible to me. In ten to twenty seconds he's off and running to the next important thing, but leaving a moment, a memory, a gift—more for me than for him, I'm sure.

If I take a phone call and don't push away from the computer, trying to continue to write or read or email, to be in two places at once, the person on the line knows instantly, asking if something is wrong. In our voices, eye contact, body language, through every nuance and gesture we are telling everyone how important they are to us with the amount of our presence we are willing to give. Sometimes choosing to be present is as simple as choosing to turn our heads and fully focus and listen, and sometimes it requires everything we can summon within ourselves to really be with someone. Being here physically is only a gift when we are also present—content to be where we are and not trying to be anywhere else. We all instantly know the difference.

The founder of a non-profit organization who has worked with under-privileged children for over thirty years is always telling me that all we really have to do is to keep showing up—in just the showing up, time after time and year after year, things happen. We are geared to focus on agenda, planning, and results. But as important as those may be, the greatest part, the most important part, the part without which all else is meaningless—is mere presence.

If we're present, things happen. If we're present, love is communicated. If we're present, God's presence becomes firm to the touch.

◐ ◑ ⊕ ⊕ ⊘

From Brother Lawrence:

> Men invent means and methods of coming at God's love, they learn rules and set up devices to remind them of that love, and it seems like a world of trouble to bring oneself into the consciousness of God's presence. Yet it might be so simple. Is it not quicker and easier just to do our common business wholly for the love of him?

In seventeenth century France, a young soldier fighting the Thirty Years War stood staring at a barren tree in the dead of winter. Stripped of leaves and flowers and fruit, it looked as lifeless as the armored figure before it—arthritic sticks reaching senselessly into a cold sky. But it was at this moment that the "fact of God" first flashed in upon that soldier's soul as he realized that what only appeared dead was full of the presence of patient life just waiting for the abundance of spring...that God's promised presence, nowhere to be seen on a gray battlefield, still flowed vibrantly just beneath the surface of gnarled bark and distressed metal—awaiting only the slightest suggestion or invitation to burst outward into extravagant life and color.

A few years later, the young soldier traded armor for the habit of a Carmelite monastery and took the name *Lawrence of the Resurrection*. A poor man with no formal education, Brother Lawrence was assigned to the kitchen, the room furthest from the chapel and spiritual center of the priory, the place where the cooking and cleaning and endless tedious tasks would drive anyone's sensation of God's presence right into the ground. Yet it was there in his kitchen as on a winter battlefield that Lawrence realized how the presence of patient life flowed just as swiftly among his pots and pans as anywhere else in his little world.

> The time of business does not with me differ from the time of prayer, and in the noise and clatter of my kitchen, while several persons are at the same time calling for different things, I possess God in as great tranquility as if I were upon my knees at the blessed sacrament... Lord of all pots and pans and things...make me a saint by getting meals and washing up the plates!

Lawrence began to actually resent the formal times of prayer and worship because they took him away from the place where he served and connected with his brothers at the most fundamental level, the place where he could lose himself in his work and the presence of God he felt so thickly: "I have quitted all forms of devotion and set prayers but those to which my state obliges me..." And he was quoted as saying:

> It was a great delusion to think that the times of prayer ought to differ from other times...that when the appointed times of prayer were past, he found no difference, because he still continued with God, praising and blessing Him with all his might, so that he passed his life in continual Joy...

Lawrence spent nearly every moment of the rest of his life within the walls of his priory, working ceaselessly at his cooking and cleaning until old age forced him to mend shoes instead.

We ought not to be weary of doing little things for the love of God, who regards not the greatness of the work, but the love with which it is performed... Nor is it needful that we should have great things to do...we can do little things for God; I turn the cake that is frying on the pan for love of him... It is enough for me to pick up but a straw from the ground for the love of God.

His entire life was lived in obscurity and poverty; he never taught or traveled or wrote anything down other than a few letters to those who recognized in him the presence of someone who had learned to be truly present to God. Yet those letters and conversations recorded by others were bound into a little book, *The Practice of the Presence of God*—now a spiritual classic read by millions to this day.

As we run in all directions at once building cathedrals and empires for God, Brother Lawrence, whom we would never have given a second glance amid the grease and fires of his kitchen, quietly carries on: simply living Kingdom instead of trying to build it. By being fully present to everyone and everything around him, no matter how seemingly insignificant or distasteful, he found the presence of God everywhere and anywhere he was.

Our sanctification does not depend upon our changing our works, but upon our doing that for God's sake which commonly we do for our own... There is not in the world a kind of life more sweet and delightful than that of a continual walk with God. Those only can comprehend it who practice and experience it...

⊙ ⊙ ⊕ ⊕ ⊘

There are stars beneath our feet.

I remember as a kid, lying in bed at night trying to process the elements of the Baltimore Catechism the nuns had recited for us that day in school—God is, God always was, God always will be... God is and God always will be were easy enough; I could picture a line beginning with the rumpled sheets on my bed and extending off forever, never ending. But *always was?* How does anyone picture that? How does anyone imagine something that has no beginning, that has always been, that always was before anything else that ever was?

It's disorienting, disturbing, irreconcilable—just like the stars beneath our feet. We are relatively comfortable with the notion of infinity over our heads, of infinite number and extension in *that* direction...in one direction only. But there should be solid ground beneath us, something we can count on, stand on. The presence of stars beneath us, the view of a starfield that is always the same wherever we look, can wither our sense of place and self if we refuse to make friends with the reality of life. We can live bewildered and defensive lives trying to maintain the illusion of solid ground, of God and stars coming at us from only one direction, relegating God's presence to neatly defined times and places—or we can let go and open up, freefalling into an endless, chaotic, riot of stars.

The presence of God burns beneath our feet, all around in every possible direction, equal density and distribution. It never changes and never dims. But we won't see it beneath us, our view remains blocked as long as we're focused on the big ball we're standing on. Neither will we see it above and around as long as the nearby star of our own consciousness floods every corner of our minds and hides it behind a blue curtain. But it's there all the same, trying to break through our defenses to tell us, "I love you enough that being with you is my highest priority—I created a universe in which I can always say yes to you everywhere, everywhen, and without exception."

God's infiniteness makes such a statement possible.

And it's here that a humble cook comes to our rescue. We've spent our whole lives searching for God out there among the stars, looking up into the distant heavens, when we should have been looking right under our feet, at the nearest face, the next task. If

God isn't present in every face and footstep, he certainly won't be present among the stars. Presence is immediate and immanent or it's not present at all.

Brother Lawrence left a trail of breadcrumbs leading directly to the realization that we enter the presence of God in no other way than by simply becoming present ourselves to everything and everyone around us. There's never been any other way. Meditation, prayer, rituals and liturgies, musical worship, prayer beads, mantras, even yoga and other physical regimens all are techniques designed to quiet the conscious mind, that part of us that talks to us, that thinks about our thoughts, the voice in our minds that takes us up and out of the present moment and into the past or the future or the abstract. Quieting that voice is like setting the sun of our consciousness so the stars can come out against a dark sky, so we can finally see the Presence everywhere around us. But techniques are just that: techniques and strategies to be used at specific times and places. What about all those moments in between?

This is the genius of Brother Lawrence's breadcrumbs, that there is never a moment we need to be outside or unaware of the presence of God, that we can enter God's presence at will, that anytime, anyplace, we can see the *shekinah*, God's tangible presence for the Hebrews, the pillar of fire by night and of cloud by day. That we can get to the point where the strategies we used to employ, the specific times of prayer and worship, become themselves the distractions, the breaks between living our lives as the uninterrupted experience of God.

When we turn off the cell phone and really enter into a conversation with a friend; when we push away from our work and look into our child's eyes or the eyes of a co-worker and really see them, hear them, help them; when we pull off the road on the way home to watch the last rays of the sun disappear over the horizon; drop our briefcase or purse at the door and take the nearest face in our hands and kiss it; when we picture the people who will benefit from whatever work we do, and then do that work better, the best we can, with their faces to guide us; when we engage everything and everyone as if God were intimately present, we are finally beginning to know the truth that will make us free. Because the truth is, God is and God always was and God always will be present—as present as we can stand him to be.

Think of the happiest moments of your life, those peak moments that stand head and shoulders above the rest. What were you doing? Who were you with? Close your eyes and see the scene—if it's one of the moments I'm talking about, it should be right there in living color. A wedding, a birth, a sunset, a face, a kiss, a quiet moment... What were you thinking at such a moment? What were you feeling? Such moments are moments when we are so completely pulled into the presence of everything around us that the borders of who we think we are, the edges of everything we think makes us separate and distinct from everyone and everything else, dissolve away and leave us naked in the Garden once more. Borderless. Finite, but having no edge. The voice in our head is mercifully silenced and God has a chance to speak—not in words but in a deep sense of connection and profound well-being.

God speaks in the language of Unity—not in English or Aramaic, but a language beneath our feet, beneath anything that can be thought to ourselves or expressed to another. Sometimes we can't hear a thing. And that hurts. But when the repeated experience of trust kicks back in, we remember that Presence is still present and can't ever be anything else. That when we're ready to hear again, the sense of connectedness, of sweetness, of joy are God's words to us with no loss in translation; they are both the things of which the presence of God is made and the sensation of its experience.

When we create connections with each other, when we see the connections between us and each other and therefore God, when we hear the language of Unity vibrating through all creation, we're not simply creating happy moments or pleasant feelings:

We are practicing the presence of God.
We are learning to fall among the stars beneath our feet.

CHALLENGE
The exact center of God's presence is the only position that exists;
no ritual can take us to Presence; it can only make us aware we already are.

Resisting evil is our duty as people of faith;
contentment comes from doing our duty, defending our faith.

Lines in the Sand

CONTENTMENT

I have sold the book which told me
to sell all that I had and give to the poor.
Serapion

AN INTERESTING THING ABOUT A SAND DUNE FIELD IS THAT IT IS
always in motion, but it never moves. The dunes themselves are
always in motion like waves in a slow motion sea, but the geology
that makes the dunes possible is fixed in the bedrock topography of
the earth with definable boundaries, like a body of water. A dune
field, like a lake or an ocean, will always be right where you left it,
but different each time you visit.

Dunes build up and erode and march across the field as the wind
has its way with them, but as old dunes fade off the leeward edge,
new dunes arise to windward, keeping the procession full at all
times—ducks in a shooting gallery gliding across, dropping down one
side, only to pop back up again on the other. And all the beautiful
lines drawn in the sand by the interplay of wind, friction, and gravity
twist and bend, constantly wrapping themselves around each other
while still remaining rooted in the topography that gives them life.

Dunes move according to rules that are not immediately apparent. There is no definable track upon which they ride; their actions
seem chaotic, unpredictable, even random, as they flow and shift—

but with a longer view, there is also an underlying logic that permits a centeredness, reliability, and a sense of place and purpose to accrue over time. Dunes move like spirit, leaving no trace of their track across the desert floor, without obvious laws and regulations governing them, without apparent destination pulling them on or even a sense of motion at all—the dune-journey always appearing as tableau, still life, a snapshot capturing a single moment without beginning or end, just an endless middle.

⊙ ⊙ ⊕ ⊕ ⊘

Living among the dunes of Egypt, Judea, and Sinai, the ancient Desert Fathers and Mothers developed dune-ish traditions preserved in their sayings such as this one told by Henri Nouwen in *The Way of the Heart*:

> Of Abba Ammonas, a disciple of Anthony, it is said that in his solitude he "advanced to the point where his goodness was so great that he took no notice of wickedness." Thus, having become bishop, someone brought a young girl who was pregnant to him, saying, "See what the unhappy wretch has done; give her a penance." But he, having marked the young girl's womb with the sign of the cross, commanded that six pairs of fine linen sheets should be given her, saying, "It is for fear that, when she comes to give birth, she may die, she or the child, and have nothing for the burial." But her accusers resumed, "Why did you do that? Give her a punishment." But he said to them, "Look brothers, she is near to death; what am I to do?" Then he sent her away and no old man dared to accuse anyone anymore.

What are we to make of someone who takes "no notice of wickedness?" How are we to react when all our rules of moral engagement are violated? What does it even mean to say that someone has become so identified with goodness that he or she can no longer see wickedness? Isn't that a contradiction in terms? Is it even possible? And if so, is it desirable, honorable, ethical? After all, aren't we supposed to be battling wickedness wherever we find it? By our religious rules, the spiritual life *is* the notice of, the avoidance of, and the condemnation of wickedness...as if the destruction of wickedness in each other and ourselves were the greatest good we could achieve.

At the same time, we crave contentment—happiness or joy, we usually call it—but we continue to resist the dune-ish qualities rooted deep beneath our feet that would give it life. As if marking our territory, we draw the lines of what we believe is essential and exclusive in our faith on the surface of the sand right where the *ruha*—wind, breath, spirit—of God blows incessantly against them. Then we spend the rest of our time defending those lines, trying to maintain them, while the dunes sail on by in the breeze. And fully engrossed in the business of guarding lines in blowing sand, we wonder why we find so little contentment.

It's not that there are no lines that are absolute; there absolutely are. But those lines don't occur at the surface; that which is essential and absolute is also so fundamental and profound as to be fixed in bedrock. There are both lines and logic that hold our faith and ethics in place, but we won't see them in the sand, and we certainly don't defend them. They are as beyond defense as they are beyond our sightlines, requiring neither defense nor apology nor even explanation. They are etched in God's domain, in the Logos beneath our feet that gives shape to every created thing regardless of our acceptance or approval.

The end of resistance is the beginning of contentment.

It is so consummately human of us to passionately resist the very principles that would nourish the contentment we just as passionately seek every waking minute of our lives.

Contentment begins with acceptance. It begins with our acceptance of God's deep, unseen lines and the relinquishment of our own on the surface, with letting surface lines be surface deep, constantly bending and wrapping themselves around each other in merciful embrace while remaining bound securely within the field of God's love.

Love always trumps lines...

Any rule, regulation, or restriction written to preserve love *only ends up preserving law* if love is not allowed to break it whenever necessary to preserve itself. For any of us trying to live the law of love, written laws won't be understood as absolute, but as guidance toward making a loving choice in each situation. To understand this is the beginning of contentment. To stop defending lines and start blowing freely within the field of love, to watch our lines dance in the sand, to begin hearing the music to which they move, is a pretty good definition of contentment itself.

More plainly: we can't create rules and codes or even interpretations of the laws we ascribe to God himself and then obey our way into contentment. We can't obey our way into contentment any more than we can obey Yeshua's Way into Kingdom because contentment is the *sensation of Kingdom*—what Kingdom feels like—and Kingdom is not governed by our lines in the sand, but by the shape of the bedrock deep beneath them.

Dancing to music only they heard, waves of men and women began drifting into the deserts of Egypt, Palestine, and Arabia in the fourth century CE. It was a movement and direction that on the surface seemed random and inexplicable, because these Desert Fathers and Mothers, as they are known to us today, were fleeing to the solitude of the desert to find God at a time when the entire

Roman world was supposedly finding God without ever leaving the comforts of home. In the fourth century, Roman emperors became Christian, religious tolerance was declared, and institutional persecution outlawed. And throughout the fourth century the Christian church was being ever more aligned with Roman power on its way to becoming the state religion that it was by the end of the century.

These were heady times for the church. The first church councils were being convened to decide issues of theology and to set the canon of the New Testament Scriptures. New Biblical manuscripts were being commissioned to be copied and new churches were being built or being repurposed out of pagan temples. The cross was quickly becoming the preeminent symbol of the church and salvation and of course temporal power. It was a time when all the Christian winds seemed to be blowing toward Rome and Constantinople, toward Antioch and Alexandria and the other major centers of commerce and religious life in the empire.

Yet it was at this moment that the Desert Fathers and Mothers chose to leave. And though their movement may have appeared to have been a sailing against the prevailing winds, there was a deeper imperative ordering their movements and direction. They believed, as Thomas Merton describes in *The Wisdom of the Desert*, that the Roman world was a "shipwreck from which each single individual man had to swim for his life...to let oneself drift along, passively accepting the tenets and values of what they knew as society, was purely and simply a disaster." That this society was now becoming aligned and allied with the church only "strengthened them in their resolve." As Merton writes,

It should seem to us much stranger than it does, this paradoxical flight from the world that attained its greatest dimensions (I almost said frenzy) when the "world" became officially Christian. These men seemed to have thought as a few rare modern thinkers...have thought, that there is really no such thing as a "Christian state."

And weren't they were right? There is no such thing as a Christian state or a Christian company or even a Christian church. There are churches, companies, and maybe even states made of Christians, but an institution cannot be anything but an institution—an organization with rules and assets and governing authority; it has no spiritual, ethical, or moral valence at all apart from the people who call it home.

The ancient Desert Fathers and Mothers knew that the intertwining of politics and culture with religion would only compromise their spirituality making it almost impossible to distinguish themselves from the background noise. And so they left. They created both communities of hermits living on their own in loose proximity to each other and communities of "cenobites" living together under a common rule of conduct and a common roof. They left their cities to literally and physically strip from their lives everything that they suspected wasn't Kingdom in order to find what really was. Legends about them contain colorful tales of battling dragons and demons as an attempt to convey the terrible internal struggle that occurs when anyone really tries to cut all the way to the bone, dig all the way to bedrock, answer the most fundamental questions of identity.

Alone, in the dark, with everything we do and say, everything we have accomplished or amassed thrust aside, what is it that is left? Who are we really? The Desert Fathers and Mothers found out—the ones that weren't driven mad by the solitude and silence—and it changed them. They learned that their identity, who they were at root, even the question itself, was meaningless except in the presence of God, in the context of relationship. Relationship with God and each other was the only relevance, significance, or meaning that there was to be found anywhere, and to ask such questions outside that Presence was not only pointless, but literally maddening.

As these desert people became more attuned to this sole Source of significance and meaning, they became more identified with it. And as they became more identified with it, whatever they had brought with them into the desert began sinking into the sands until all that was left of them looked like God-love, thought like God-love, acted like God-love...and took no notice of wickedness.

There is a story of a hermit who was attacked by robbers in the desert. After being rescued by his fellow hermits, they rounded up the robbers and took them to the authorities in the nearest town to be thrown in jail. But after speaking with their Abbot, the monks were so remorseful they broke into the jail that night and released the prisoners from the torturers.

Or this one translated by Merton from the *Verba Seniorum,* the Sayings of the Elders:

> One of the monks of Scete committed a grave error, and the wisest hermit was called upon to judge him. The hermit refused, but they insisted so much that in the end he agreed to go. He arrived carrying on his back a bucket with holes in it, out of which poured sand.
>
> "I have come to judge my neighbor," said the hermit to the head of the convent. "My sins are pouring out behind me, like the sand running from this bucket. But since I don't look back, and pay no attention to my own sins, I was called upon to judge my neighbor!" The monks called a halt to the punishment immediately.

Abbot Anthony, the founder of the monastic movement and father of all hermits "taught Abbot Ammonas, saying: 'You must advance yet further in the fear of God.' And taking him out of the cell he showed him a stone, saying: 'Go and insult that stone and beat it without ceasing.' When this had been done, Anthony asked him if the stone had answered back. 'No,' said Ammonas. Then Abbot Anthony said, 'You too must reach the point where you no longer take offense at anything.'"

It is said that Anthony came to the conclusion that the devil himself was not "purely evil, since God could not create evil, and all his works are good." So to Anthony, even the devil himself still had "some good in him." For these desert people, when identification with Unity was full enough, it was almost impossible to regress to or even recall the separation and division that used to define their lives:

> There were two elders living together in a cell, and they had never had so much as one quarrel with one another. One therefore said to the other: "Come on, let us have at least one quarrel, like other men." The other said: "I don't know how to start a quarrel." The first said: "I will take this brick and place it here between us. Then I will say: It is mine. After that you will say: It is mine. This is what leads to a dispute and a fight." So then they placed the brick between them, one said: "It is mine, and the other replied to the first: I do believe that it is mine." The first one said again: "It is not yours, it is mine." So the other answered: "Well then, if it is yours, take it!" Thus they did not manage after all to get into a quarrel.

To be clear, taking no notice of wickedness is describing more the inward attitude toward the wickedness we encounter rather than the outward response to it. It's an attitude that essentially says, "The wickedness I find in you, is the wickedness I find in myself; how do we row out of these waters together in our little boat?" At the same time, the innocent must still be protected against aggression, and unlawfulness must be judged institutionally for the greater good, but how a person responds inwardly to abuse and injustice without allowing offendability to drive emotion and behavior to the point of diminishing returns—diminished community and love—meant everything to the spirituality of the desert people and their sense of contentment.

There is an amazing freedom and contentment in taking no notice of wickedness: to be so identified with God and each other that even the interior and exterior space between brothers and sisters breaks down, that every person encountered is not seen as an object to which either good or bad things can be "done," but simply as an extension of self. This is exactly what loving your neighbor as yourself really means. Love is not anything that can be done or accomplished at all, but is simply identification itself, the unity and connection with the beloved.

Again from Merton:

Love in fact *is* the spiritual life, and without it all the other exercises of the spirit, however lofty, are emptied of content and become mere illusions. The more lofty they are, the more dangerous the illusion...Love takes one's neighbor as one's other self, and loves him with all the immense humility and discretion and reserve and reverence without which no one can presume to enter into the sanctuary of another's subjectivity... Love demands a complete inner transformation—for without this we cannot possibly come to identify ourselves with our brother. We have to become, in some sense, the person we love. And this involves a kind of death of our own being, our own self. No matter how hard we try, we resist this death: we fight back with anger, with recriminations, with demands, with ultimatums. We seek any convenient excuse to break off and give up the difficult task.

Because of this difficulty, it was the oldest and most dedicated Fathers and Mothers who had learned to live this Way of Yeshua and served as models for the rest. "Abbot Joseph asked Abbot Pastor: 'Tell me how I can become a monk.' The elder replied: 'If you want to have rest here in this life and also in the next, in every conflict with another say: Who am I? And judge no one.'"

The sayings of the Desert Fathers and Mothers preserved in ancient texts are full of the actions and instruction of abbots and elders as they work with the younger brothers and sisters in community. It's fascinating to watch them, to see that the issues with which they struggled seventeen hundred years ago in far off deserts are the same issues we battled just now on the way home from work. As different as we may be, we share this much as humans—that the enemies of their contentment then are still the enemies of our contentment today. In all their mythical battles, dragons and demons were never vanquished for all time, but only immediately and for the wielder of the sword alone. We must all battle those same dragons for ourselves before we can ever become characterized by contentment.

� � ⊕ ⊕ ⊕

Dragons are the symbols that the ancients used to represent intense spiritual struggle; we would probably use a different image today, but though dragons may seem archaic to us, the struggles they represent are as near as our next breath. Dragons steal our contentment by focusing our attention on ourselves as separate and distinct from each other, from the Unity and oneness that takes no notice of another's wickedness—by encouraging us to obsess over the lines we imagine exist between us and each other rather than letting those lines dissipate in the wind.

The dragons among us are the illusions we put in place to hide ourselves from ourselves—the distractions and notions of who we think we are, the bits of acquired relevance, power, and celebrity that mask the nothingness that exists apart from God and each other. To battle them successfully is to let them fall away, leaving us at last and again naked in the Garden waiting patiently to see Who shows up. But successful or not, we must all do battle: if we don't take the battle to the dragons, the dragons bring the battle to us, and for most of us, this is exactly what happens.

By choosing not to fight, we live our lives as if the dragons are real, and our lives become defined by dragons instead of Presence. But dragons have no power that we don't give them, and as old age, sickness, financial insecurity, or eventual death catches up to us, one by one the dragons of relevance, power, and celebrity are vanquished anyway as we lose the power or will to sustain them. When we are not willing to give up our illusions, illusions are taken from us by time and attrition; the choice between nothingness and Presence cannot be avoided—we all must choose eventually or eventually hit the bottom of nothingness asserting itself in the absence of a choice for Presence.

But instead of waiting to hit bottom in their noisy cities, the desert people fled to the silence of the wilderness as a way of bringing the bottom up to hit them. By purposefully casting aside all their illusions rather than waiting for time and age and circumstance to do it for them, they accelerated the process and found themselves being transformed by it at the same time.

The Desert Fathers and Mothers didn't flee to the desert because they were antisocial or unconcerned with the plight of others: there was more genuine society in their remote enclaves than in the crowded cities from which they fled. They left their communities in order to discover what living in community really meant, and as with Abbot Anthony, when the silence of the desert had truly filled his heart, he came back to the cities, bringing his silence with him to work among the people once again. Or as Merton put it:

> The Coptic hermits who left the world as though escaping from a wreck, did not merely intend to save themselves. They

knew that they were helpless to do any good for others as long as they floundered about in the wreckage. But once they got a foothold on solid ground, things were different. Then they had not only the power but even the obligation to pull the whole world to safety after them.

Abbot Anthony said: "The prayer of the monk is not perfect until he no longer realizes himself or the fact that he is praying."

This is really the kernel of Yeshua's Way. We think we need to constantly emphasize the spirituality of every event rather than allow ourselves to become immersed enough to forget it; to call out and segregate sacred times and places rather than blur and blend every time and place into a seamless whole; to constantly monitor and evaluate our spiritual progress and achievement rather than to lose ourselves in the give and take of daily relationship; to think about everything instead of living it—to divide and conquer rather than connect and submit. To the hermits of the desert, life was nothing that could be thought or spoken or written down:

"One of the monks, called Serapion, sold his book of the gospels and gave the money to those who were hungry, saying: 'I have sold the book which told me to sell all that I had and give to the poor.'" What need is there even for the text of Scripture, once its truth is written on our hearts?

In the desert there is no pretense. There is no lofty theology or abstraction. There is sun and sand and a day's work for a day's sustenance. Life is simple because the line between life and death has been scraped so thin as to be nearly invisible. In the place where everything has been stripped to subsistence, there is no time for or interest in those things that glitter and attract, but have no intrinsic value. A drop of water is infinitely more valuable than a brick of gold: one has the power to preserve life and the other does not, and knowing the difference makes all the difference. There is just life and death and whatever happens in between—the endless procession of dunes.

Contentment is like a sand dune. It will utterly disrespect and disregard any lines we draw to define its shape and scope: anything we think it is, expect it to be, or try to create will simply blow through our fingers as it swirls over the next crest and down the slip face beyond. Contentment plays by no rules we can write down and constantly violates the ones we do. Rooted and bounded only by the shape of love, the topography deep down under the sands, contentment moves about, marching and dancing in the breath of God's wind, appearing random only until we learn to see with our Father's eyes.

There is no contentment apart from this second sight that comes from letting sand be sand and do what sand does. Nothing we build and defend or indict and resist—no rightness, righteousness, cause, mission, belief, or faith will make us content unless rooted in the unoffendability of true connection and identity.

We can ride the dunes of contentment like slow motion surfers on nearly frozen waves. We can release our lines and allow love to dictate the motion of our lives in ways that violate all our rules of what is and what should be, or we can hold our ground, defend our lines as the dunes march on by. But whatever we choose, the wonderful thing about dunes is that there is always another one coming right behind the one that just passed, always another crest behind the present trough in which we find ourselves.

No matter how many dunes we let pass, we can always catch the next one—if we're simply willing to let go of our lines in the sand and blow freely about on God's breath in the infinite field of his love.

The field is always full, always changing, always in motion, but always silent and still as well—the snapshot of a single moment. There is no anticipated destination and no clinging memory in contentment: it always was and always will be, and we can only enter it from its endless middle.

CHALLENGE

Contentment never comes from reinforcing distinctions;
it is the sensation of a release of personal boundaries, becoming unoffendable.

TRADITION
*God has a perfect plan for every human life:
God's will and destiny for each of us.*

The Fat End of the Telescope

DESTINY

If I ever go looking for my heart's desire again, I won't look any
further than my own back yard. Because if it isn't there,
I never really lost it to begin with.

L. Frank Baum

DESTINY IS A SLIPPERY SUBJECT. IT REFUSES TO LIE STILL LIKE A
corpse on an autopsy table, but is always popping up here and there
like one of those arcade games where you try to hit the head appearing in a grid of holes with a big hammer. Is it a chicken or an egg, a
forest or a tree, a wave or a particle, both, none, something in between? It's much more subject than object, much more art than
science: and like art, it says much more about the beholder than the
beholden, more about who's looking and how than what is really
there. When we see destiny, what do we really see—the one and only
absolute future or our own desire as in a mirror's reflection?

Quantum mechanics tells us we can never really observe anything
purely anyway—observer always gets mixed up with the observed,
subject with object—the experiment is always changed by the observation of the experimenter and the terms and nature of the experiment.
Like a person who knows he or she is on camera: would they have
really done this or said that, struck a particular pose if no one was
watching, recording? We can never know once the picture is taken,

the pose set; the snapshot in our hand was destined to be, if for no other reason than because it is there in our hand, destined to be.

Destiny is like this. Does it really exist? One of those fantastic, top-heavy rock formations in a Southwest desert looks destined to fall—has to at some point as gravity has its way. At the moment you look, it certainly has the *potential* to fall, but is potential the same as destiny? Did that rock have that same potential when it was still part of a vast and ancient plain, before wind and water carved it into a fantastic sculpture with an apparent destiny? We see the destiny now; would we have seen it then? Was there any other course that wind and water could have taken?

We may say a gifted child is destined for greatness. After the fact, we certainly do say that great people were destined to be where they are today or were in history, but were they really? Gifted children disappoint or die young, and others you never saw coming rise up to take their places. Is it still destiny if we never saw it coming? And if we can't see it coming, what good is it? If it never offers a clue beforehand, what does it mean to say it was destiny afterhand?

A concept like destiny is only as good as our ability to discern it, to know what it is in the unfolding so we can aid and abet it in our lives or the lives of others. If we know our destiny, we can help it along—but if it's really destiny, does it need our help? Won't it just happen no matter what we do or fail to do? Isn't that part of the definition of destiny after all?

We have an odd way of looking at life, as if effects are in fact their own causes. A certain effect has been realized, therefore it was always meant to be; any of the series of causes that led to the final effect were only means to the end of that effect that was, in effect, its own cause—its destiny.

◌ ◍ ◎ ◉ ⊕

One of the staples of today's media is the celebrity bio—hour-plus-long documentaries on the life of someone who currently has the nation's attention on a string. It doesn't matter whether the person has contributed in any substantive or positive way to culture or society, only whether the producers believe enough people will devote an hour-plus of their lives to watch the life of an actor, model, businessperson, politician, or other such figure unfold before them.

The presentations follow a predictable pattern: after flashy opening graphics, music, and images of the celebrity being celebrated, the frames roll back to grainy black and white stills and 8mm home movies of a non-descript child in whose unfamiliar features we strain to see the contours of the famous face to be. There's an undeniable fascination in seeing these powerful and ubiquitous people reduced to a moment when they were as powerless as any other child born into this world—as apparently unaware of the trajectory of their future as we are of our own. But then a camera crew is inevitably sent to an obscure nursing home somewhere in Nebraska to interview the third grade teacher of the now-famous celebrity who invariably says something to the effect that she just knew that this child was going to be important someday because he or she was so intelligent or talented, had this or that other special quality, or in some way displayed the discernable seeds of greatness.

Whether she actually thought that at the time is much less important than how she remembers it now. The fact is, the child she knew is now a powerful celebrity: the end result is known, so all the moments in between are seen as just means to the end in which we're standing. Effect becomes its own cause as all those moments, all those lifelong details take on new significance and meaning in light of the end result. There is a sense of inevitability and predetermination to individual events: each choice is reinterpreted as a significant milestone along the way toward greatness; each crushing failure or defeat is transformed into just another hurdle that was ultimately surmounted—that had to have been surmounted—a badge of courage and perseverance drained of whatever frustration or despair might have been felt at the time. In other words, there is the sense that everything *had* to happen just this way, because it *did* happen just this way.

We apply this peculiar way of looking at life to everyone including ourselves; it's just much more dramatic in the life of someone who has risen head and shoulders above the crowd. When something happens, it was "meant to be;" when something doesn't happen, it "wasn't meant to be." Either way, it is still "God's will." We speak of the one and only person who was born to be our husband or wife and has been waiting to meet us since birth, as if all of life and time exists out there somewhere in its entirety like a gigantic reel of motion picture film playing itself out in the theatres of our consciousness.

The moment in which we're standing right now is always at the tail end of the entire string of moments we call our lives. Each moment we experience, as if in the circle-frame of a telescope panning the horizon, slides into our awareness out of precognitive-blackness and slips back out of view into memory-blackness as the circle moves on. But even though no longer in view, those once-viewed moments can be recalled and cataloged, the dots connected into a traceable path to this moment—footprints on the beach or stepping-stones in the lawn. Against our memory's backdrop of all the paths not taken, the one that *was* taken stands out in luminous relief as the one and only path to our present moment. But was it really one and only, inevitable, destined to be?

○ ① ⊕ ⊕ ⊕

It's like looking through the fat end of a telescope... Watch a boy with a telescope; at some point he just has to turn it around and look through the fat end. Didn't you? When you look through the skinny end, the end you're supposed to look through, what you get is a lot of detail but a very narrow field of vision—the more powerful the scope the more detail you get, but always at the expense of breadth of vision, like looking through smaller and smaller knotholes in a fence. In other words, you can see quite a lot of very little. But when you turn it around and look through the fat end, what you see is like looking down a dark tunnel to a small circle of light that contains a wide field of vision compressed into fish-eyed distortion, like a reflection in a bubble or one of those convex mirrors that lets you see around corners. The fat end lets you see very little of quite a lot.

As with telescopes, so is life. We look at our lives as through a telescope that is always pointed one way—toward the future. When we look back at our past, we're looking through the fat end and seeing the wide view of all our moments together at once compressed down into a fish-eyed whole—a distorted view, with the distortion being the sense of inevitability that comes from knowing the present moment to which they have all led. Everything had to happen this way, because it did happen this way, and really for no other reason.

But when we turn to face the future and look through the skinny end, detail increases as field of vision decreases, becoming so pinhole narrow as to allow us to see nothing but one framed moment at a time. Which moment? The only one we can ever see: this moment, the one in which we're standing right now with a choice in hand that will directly affect the next moment, the one we can't see coming. Looking back we see all our moments at once, looking forward, we can see only one, and that is truly maddening. We tremble at the thought of all those unknown future moments coming at us from out there in the dark, like swimming in the ocean at night with unknown creatures layered somewhere below us in the black water, rows of razor teeth coming up unseen out of the depths.

Scared to death, we try in every way we can imagine to widen our field of vision through the skinny end, to see more moments stringing out before us in the future the way they do out behind us in the past. Whether we dream of time machines, have our palms or tarot cards read, pray for clarity or for God to make his will known to us—it all comes from the same place: we want to see more moments.

But this is where our distorted view through the fat end of the telescope may be blinding us to the true nature of things. Since the view of moments past, the path taken, looks linear and connected like a route on a map, we assume that our future path would look the same if we could just get a glimpse. As if our future is all laid out and just waiting for us to follow its predestined track. How much easier life would be if only we could see that shape.

Misunderstanding the nature of time and space, we think of the universe as containing a vast amount of empty space into which galaxies, stars, planets, all the physical matter we observe are expanding. But according to our brightest scientific minds, this is not so. There is no space beyond the physical matter we can see; space is *defined* by the matter that occupies it—or, space simply doesn't exist until a physical body exists to define the space around it. If our universe is expanding, then space is expanding with it, with nothing we could call space beyond.

It's the same with time. We think of the universe as containing a vast amount of time into which we move, our lives occupying a small segment of unknown duration. But this would not be so either. There is no time beyond the present moment existing out there somewhere and waiting for us to enter. Time exists as space exists, defined by the matter and consciousness that occupy it; there is no time beyond what we experience in this moment—or, there is essentially just one moment, the herenow moment, always.

What we think of as the future existing somewhere out there in a straight line from here, doesn't exist at all until the moment it becomes the present. It's as if the present moment creates the future by expanding into it and making it the present; instead of a single future path to follow, that with which we are really presented is an infinite number of possible futures, a cloud of possible moments, any of which we could step into, making that possible moment the reality of the present. Our choices determine which possible moment becomes the next present moment—or should I say determines the new conditions of the continuous present moment. And each choice we make creates a whole new set of possible futures, or better, a new vantage point from which a different cloud of possible moments becomes visible.

This is how we really live our lives: as one moment—one continuous moment—with a continuous flow of choices that constantly determines the conditions of our moment as well as the next set of choices. Looked at this way, we're not moving into a preexisting future; we're creating the future one choice at a time. Both past and future don't exist at all except as thoughts, memories, electrical impulses in our brains.

All that really is, is herenow.

The point I'm trying to make is not that there is no destiny or that God can't or doesn't know the "future," but that whatever God knows or plans is never *experienced* by us in any other way than as one continuous moment.

Whenever you see a movie for the first time, you experience it frame by frame in suspenseful excitement. The fact that millions of other people may already know how it comes out—from writers, producers, actors, crewmembers, editors, marketers, critics, to other movie goers—in no way dampens your experience of the unfolding story as long as no one tells you the ending. If you record a sporting event to watch later and stay away from all sports news, you can experience it as if it were happening live even though the whole world already knows the outcome.

What God may know about time and destiny has nothing to do with how we experience the time of our lives, and to think of our future as extending any further than the choice we hold in our hands right now is to cloud our chance of ever really experiencing Yeshua's Way to Kingdom.

○ ◑ ⊕ ⊕ ⊘

Just as we confuse subject with object, cause with effect, and potential with destiny, we also confuse God's will with the future. We tend to think of God's will, destiny, and the future as synonymous: God knows the future, has a perfect plan (a will) for our lives, which by definition then becomes a destiny.

A counseling pastor once told me about the question he gets most often from people in their sessions with him: "What is God's will for my life?" Translation: "What is God's perfect plan for my life, my future and destiny?" When we pray for clarity or for God to show us his will, we're really asking to be shown more moments, our future, the future we believe already exists out there somewhere in God's perfect plan. But if we believe that God has a will, a plan, a destiny for each of us, then that plan is the one-and-only perfect plan that represents the ideal life we could lead for him, for ourselves, and everyone we touch.

God knows this plan, but he's not telling, so our job is to try to discover the plan by whatever means necessary and with minimal help from God, and execute it perfectly—or our lives will always be less than...God planned. Talk about pressure—or talk about resentment: if God already has it all mapped out, why won't he just tell us so we can get on board and start pulling in the same direction?

Knowing "God's will" becomes a tool, a euphemism, for prognostication, for knowing the future, for removing risk from our decisions. Through prayer and prophecy, dreams and careful study of Scripture, we imagine all sorts of futures for ourselves under the guise of God's will. Some we act on, others we don't, but whether we act or not, or even are successful or not, how do we ever know the difference between our own deepest desires and a destiny or will outside of ourselves?

I received an email a while back from a friend who had launched a business that he was sure was God's will for him and his wife:

> We are in some trouble. Due to a much slower business start than we forecasted and then a terrible August, we are struggling and are six weeks behind on making our rent. Our landlord has already begun proceedings to evict us if we do not rectify the rent situation within eight days. We have exhausted our financial reserves, and are now in the cleft of the rock and really need to see the Lord.
>
> I would beg of you all to please join us here for a dedication and prayer session in which we ask the Lord to bless what we're doing here and to work a miracle for both us and the community... When we began, we *knew that we knew that we knew* that this was the new thing that God had for us. He gave it to us, and we have given it over completely to him. We have also made no secret both in our external promotion and internal attitude here that it is indeed "His baby."

My friend knew that he knew that he knew that this business was God's will, but still had to abandon it shortly after writing those words. It can be heartbreaking or self-fulfilling or anything in between when we mix our deepest yearnings and desire with our notion of God's will.

More recently, I was attending a worship-music conference at a large community church in which a pastor was attempting to plan a huge, multi-church musical worship service for the near future. He laid out his plan and vision to a room full of pastors and musicians and then asked for comments and suggestions. If you've never had the pleasure, let me tell you that musicians are generally not the least bit shy about expressing their opinions on just about any subject, but when it comes to music, it's mandatory. As the comments and suggestions turned more strident, moving into the realm of objections, a woman's hand bolted up in the middle of the room. When the pastor, who had been taking everything graciously in stride, acknowledged her, she shot out to him, "This is your vision—don't let anyone crush your vision. If someone tries to crush your vision, it's a sure sign that God is in it..."

I almost ducked waiting for the lightning bolt to strike, but instead heads started nodding up and down all over the room, and an audible murmur of approval, even hushed awe, rose and fell among us—objections immediately sliding back to a few more almost sheepish suggestions before stopping altogether. "If someone tries to crush your vision, it's a sure sign that God is in it..." I almost don't know where to start.

Maybe we were all just feeling a bit too polite that day to challenge such a statement or maybe we realized that the objections had gone a bit too far and so backed off. Possibly, but that still doesn't explain the signs and sounds of approval when there should have just been statues and crickets. And I really wanted to know, really wanted to jump up and ask how we could know for sure that God wasn't in the crushing instead of the vision, and I wanted to comment that I could think of a few visions that I was sure God would want crushed, but I'm thankful I kept my place. I doubt I would have made the smallest dent; it really was a beautifully crafted, bulletproof force field to place around anyone's desired destiny.

There's an interesting phenomenon that centers on the belief in reincarnation. When someone is describing the past lives they believe they have lived, he or she will invariably have been a princess or warrior, king or high priest, or other such romantic, idealized figure. You never really hear of anyone being the guy who swept up the camel dung from around the pyramids in a past life. Psychologically, it's not too difficult to see where this is coming from in a person's present life that is viewed as mundane, demeaning, or failing: the need for relief in the present becomes realized in the belief in a spectacular past—that this disappointing present life is only a temporary lull in the grand sweep of one's entire existence.

What is harder for us to see, though, is that what reincarnation does for the past, our notion of God's will does for the future. When people speak of God's will for their lives, it is invariably described as something spectacular and significant, as a great work or ministry for the Lord that will have far-reaching effects in the world and the lives of others. Out of our difficult circumstances and trying times in the present, we long for the relief we find in the promise of a spectacular future that God has already planned for us since before we were born, a guaranteed future for which we just have to wait to be realized in God's perfect timing.

Destiny and God's will mixed with our deepest desires and need for relief from a difficult present create a Walter Mitty-like life of living off the adrenaline of recurring fantasies at the expense of the present moment. Reincarnation focuses the heart and mind on the past; the search for God's will focuses on the future—anything to avoid living fully in the reality of herenow, the only moment that really exists, the only moment in which God's presence can be entered and from which a choice can be made to change and transform our lives.

Once again, the point is not that dreams or goals for future accomplishment should not be engaged or that they are misplaced or unreachable or unimportant, but that as an imagined expression of God's will, they miss the point entirely—and focusing on them takes us *out* of God's will by taking us out of the herenow moment—the only place God's will actually exists.

☉ ☽ ⊕ ⊕ ⊕

"My Father, if it is possible, let this cup pass from me..."

Yeshua in the Garden before his arrest, sweating blood in the present over the fear of his immediate future, praying to his Father for another outcome. How human is this? How many times have you and I been there with him, sweating blood and praying to change our circumstances, to change God's mind, for God's will to be bent to our own?

When we think of will, we think of willpower or the force of an iron will or a legal will whose authority extends even after the death of the living one. For us, will is the authority, power, force, or law that gives us the ability to choose for ourselves, to execute those choices and make them happen. Will is the ability to do what we want, to have independence and autonomy, to be the captain of our own ships. We merge will with ego, our sense of identity, and our will becomes who it is we think we are.

And when we apply this sense of "will" to God, God's will becomes the symbol of *his* identity, power, and authority—the ultimate juggernaut, an omnipotent bulldozer that flattens all other wills before it, including our own. Is it any wonder it's so difficult for us to turn our wills over to God, to accept God's will over our own, when it seems to do so is the turning over of our very identity and independence, who we are, everything we wish to be? It's much easier to imagine that what we wish to be is also God's destiny for us somewhere in the future.

"...yet not as I will, but as you will."

Prayer made simply to change God's mind or bend his will is not prayer at all: it's manipulation or negotiation, but not prayer.

To pray in Aramaic is *sela*, which means to bend toward, incline toward, heed or to listen to—it is body language that leans forward, a sense of breathless expectancy, the moment before lips touch in a first kiss or Christmas morning as the lid is pulled off the biggest box under the tree. Something is coming; something is here. Something good...

From its roots, *sela* can also mean to lay a snare for—a hunter's term. When the hunter lays the snare, he carefully clears a space, sets the trap, covers it back over with leaves and brush, then retreats to his blind where he quietly awaits the presence of his prey and sustenance, every nerve and sense tuned for the sounds that will spring him into action. The clearing of an interior space, laying a snare, setting a trap in our hearts for God, waiting breathlessly for the first kiss of his presence is *sela*. We can *sela* amid the pots and pans of a noisy kitchen, in the sanctuary of a gothic church, and without the slightest realization that we are praying at all.

Instead of trying to bend circumstance and will into a destiny of our choosing, *sela* leans into the circumstance and will that already exist herenow. God's will for us never exists in the future or the past—only in the present, because for us, God's presence can only be experienced in the present.

And what kind of will do we experience in God's presence? In Aramaic, God's will is his *sebyana*: his desire, pleasure, delight, and deepest purpose and has nothing to do with force or power or authority or legality. "...not as I will, but as you will" is not the bulldozing of Yeshua's desire and purpose, but a leaning into, an inclining toward the desire and purpose of his Father. It is an identification, a becoming one with the deepest purpose and desire that cannot be separated from who God is. We confuse our identity with our accomplishments; God never makes such a mistake.

When God says, "I am who I am," *hayah asher hayah* as recorded in Hebrew to Moses from the burning bush, who he is, *is* his deepest desire and purpose and pleasure. What is that? It is written right into his name in Aramaic, *Alaha*: unity and oneness. What does that look like? It looks and feels and sounds and tastes and acts like love. Love is unity and oneness; unity and oneness is God; God is love. Unity with God and each other is God's deepest purpose and desire, and when we make God's deepest purpose our own, we have perfected *sela*, we have entered God's will and destiny.

We look for God's will in a changed future, because we are still looking for what we need to do in order to comply with God's authority, what we need to accomplish in order to realize God's plan and destiny, but understood this way...

God's will is not a "what" at all...

There is no what to God's will; there is no one-and-only plan or accomplishment or future that defines it. There is no one specific thing we need to do to enter God's will, just as there's no one specific will for you and a different one for me; God's will is the same for everyone. God doesn't play hide and seek with his will, taunting us with the cruel promise of a plan he won't spell out. If God wants us in his will, then his will is perfectly plain.

God's will is not a "what," but a "how."

I'm becoming more and more convinced that God *doesn't much care what we do*; what we do doesn't much matter. What matters is *how* we do what we do, and anything we do will be done exactly in the center of God's will, if we do it with the right how: in unity and oneness—in love.

Mother Teresa said, "In this life we cannot do great things, we can only do small things with great love."

We want to build great cathedrals and worldwide networks; what do those mean to God's deepest purpose and desire? We want to scale great intellectual and theological mountains, earn advanced degrees; God's fingers are still drumming on his desk. We search high and low, sweat blood our entire lives looking for God's will and purpose and destiny only to find that it was always the first, middle, and last things he ever said to us—the only thing, really. Over and over, teaching after teaching, story after story, healing after healing, he has never stopped telling us that all the purpose and destiny he has ever planned is just one long embrace, a forever embrace—an embrace that holds all the oneness and unity we can have with him and each other right now.

If we can learn to stop trying to see the future through the fat end of the telescope, if we can begin to accept our lives as one moment—one continuous moment that contains everything there is or will ever be, we can begin to glimpse the true nature of our destiny. Not as some "what" out there in the darkness waiting to be realized, but as the "how" of our lives herenow.

◐ ◑ ⊕ ⊕ ⊕

But if God's will and our destiny lie not in the future but in the present, not in a what but a how, then exactly what *are* we supposed to do in this life?

Augustine of Hippo said, "Love God and do as you please."

To our legal, contractual minds, such an injunction sounds dangerously permissive, but with the right how in place—love, unity—any what will do and no what outside the rule of love would ever be attempted or even contemplated. We can't fail. Still, choices must be made continuously, so of all the possible futures before us in this moment, all of the dizzying possible moments in the cloud around our heads, how do we choose?

Joseph Campbell, the great teacher and writer on comparative religion and mythology said, "My general formula for my students is 'Follow your bliss.' Find where it is, and don't be afraid to follow it."

To our sacrificial and self-denying hearts, such a suggestion seems hopelessly selfish, but listen as he develops his thought further:

> If you do follow your bliss...the life that you ought to be living is the one you are living. Wherever you are—if you are following your bliss, you are enjoying that refreshment, that life within you, all the time. When you can see that, you begin to meet people who are in your field of bliss, and they open doors to you. I say, follow your bliss and don't be afraid, and doors will open where you didn't know they were going to be.

There is nothing at all selfish about following our bliss. As we are presented with our moment's set of choices, how do we choose? Which possible future and moment do we realize? If we use our bliss once again like a divining rod—the forked branch fabled to vibrate in the presence of water—running it across our set of choices to see where our spirit vibrates the strongest, that place, that vibration and sense of wonder, makes the choice obvious.

Following our bliss is not a choosing of our will over that of God or a bulldozing of the wills of others with our own. It's a realization of or alignment with the fact that whatever destiny we have is vibrating within us right now. The Kingdom is not out there somewhere to be found by observation, but is within, among, and in our midst. (Luke 17) Our bliss comes from God too, of course, and finding the Source of that vibration is at once universal and unique for each of us. Each of us is uniquely wired to have different likes and dislikes and skill sets and body types that will lend themselves to favoring different frequencies of vibration. No one frequency is better than any other; as in music, it takes all the frequencies together to perform the symphony.

Our bliss is our cue and clue to the frequency of our vibration, the narrowing of the set of choices before us. It's not that we don't consider others in our choices, but that we recognize that we will offer the most to any other when we are vibrating at our "destined" frequency, in our sweet spot. Doing that which we love will always make us the best lover; do that first, whenever possible, and become the widest, most transparent conduit of God's unity and love. This flow of God's love will happen automatically, effortlessly, without our even thinking about it, and when moments come in which we are overwhelmed, when all the good choices are gone and what remains is only the lesser of evils, even then in the face of all we don't know, there is always at least one thing we do know—our bliss. And that is a place to start. Joseph Campbell again:

> I came to this idea of bliss because in Sanskrit, which is the great spiritual language of the world, there are three terms that represent the brink, the jumping-off place to the ocean of transcendence: *sat-chit-ananda*. The word "*sat*" means being. "*Chit*" means consciousness. "*Ananda*" means bliss or rapture. I thought, "I don't know whether my consciousness is proper consciousness or not; I don't know whether what I know of my being is my proper being or not; but I do know where my rapture is. So let me hang on to rapture, and that will bring me both my consciousness and my being." I think it worked.

Remembering Thomas Merton's prayer: "My Lord God, I have no idea where I am going. I do not see the road ahead of me. I cannot know for certain where it will end. Nor do I really know myself, and the fact that I think that I am following your will does not mean that I am actually doing so. But I believe that the desire to please you does in fact please you."

The two thoughts are one, a Unity, of course. "Truth is one; the sages speak of it by many names," reads a line from the Rig Veda of ancient India. All wisdom is one because it has only one Source. If it's truly wise, then it is always the same story with the same message every time—only with different characters and colors to suit the storyteller's bliss.

The bliss of Campbell, the desire of Merton, the Kingdom of Yeshua, the will of the Father, are all the same thing—deepest purpose, desire, pleasure, delight—*sebyana*. When all else is gone or taken, we are never left without at least the desire for our heart's desire, no matter how remote it may seem. And that is a start—a choice point that leads to the smile point, which is all the destiny we can ever expect to experience in life.

> If I ever go looking for my heart's desire again,
> I won't look any further than my own back yard.
> Because if it isn't there, I never really lost it to begin with.
> *Dorothy, The Wizard of Oz*

Though it took Oz for Dorothy to learn this and may take us a lifetime along our own yellow road to do the same, in the end we may find that our heart's desire, God's will, was always as near as our own back yard, our next breath, the next sand dune.

There is no future to change beyond the present moment...only the choice to change the moment we're in. There is no destiny waiting in the fat end of the telescope...our destiny is always now.

CHALLENGE
God's will is not what we do, but how we do what we do:
a deepest purpose identical for everyone, a destiny that is always now.

We can be proud of finishing the race, fighting the good fight;
we will be judged on how well we overcome the challenges God gives us.

Hero

RELEASE

And the end of all our exploring will be to arrive where we
started and know the place for the first time.

T.S. Eliot

I'm not sure why we speak of the mists of time...

OR OF THE TIMES OF THE ANCIENTS AS MISTY OR DARK. I SUPPOSE IT
has to do with our inability to see them or their worlds clearly, to
penetrate the mysteries surrounding people so far removed. Even
so, it's our seeing that's misty, not their ability to be seen. I often
catch myself thinking of the first half of the twentieth century in
dramatic black and white and the last half of the nineteenth in
unsmiling sepia. Apparently it's the nature of the record people
leave behind that creates the lasting image we carry around in our
minds' eye: the legacy of the early twentieth century is bequeathed
in black and white photos and film noir, the latter nineteenth in
the sepia tones of the daguerreotype—our windows to those worlds.
Logically, we know that Fred Astaire and Ginger Rogers danced in
color, just as we know Abraham Lincoln must have smiled from
time to time, but the images they left now stand taller and truer
than whatever truth hides behind. Farther back, we have only

paintings and sculptures, coins and cave drawings to visually guide us, and then nothing at all to mark the lives that passed therethen.

Misty. Dark.

The ancient stone monuments that have survived; the temples, pyramids, and obelisks scoured by wind and sand; the broken columns of the Roman Forum or Greek Acropolis paint for us a monochromatic image of the lives of the ancients—they were anything but. Archeologists now know that the statues and buildings of ancient Egypt were brightly painted, even garishly so by our standards; Rome was awash in color. Though it's hard to imagine the stately Sphinx clothed in anything but naked stone, the ancients lived in a riot of color and texture.

We are all connected; we are all alone...

We often condescendingly think of the ancients as...ancient, as if ancient and primitive were synonymous, as if those living in antiquity were somehow not capable of knowing what we know or feeling what we feel, as if lives we view mistily from museums and books may fascinate and even inspire, but are not truly analogous to the complicated lives we lead herenow.

In truth, the ancient civilizations of the Far East, Mesopotamia, Greece, Rome, even the Americas were every bit as sophisticated as our own. In politics, commerce, art, literature, religion, warfare, personal and public relationships, in every way we identify ourselves as human, the ancients are us and we are the ancients. Reading their words, we recognize our own emotions and motivations, hopes and dreams: in their politics and warfare we see our own ambition and ruthlessness; in their commerce, our resourcefulness and greed; in their art, literature, and religion, our love of beauty, desire for perfection, and need for meaning; and in their relationships, our passion and fear of loneliness.

In only one aspect are we different—but as that one aspect reigns supreme in our culture, it colors all our perceptions. It is our technology alone that separates us from the ancients. They had chariots and catapults and handwritten messages delivered by birds or horsemen, and we have space shuttles and cell phones and laser-guided missiles. They built with stone and wood; we use metal, glass, and advanced polymers. But though one soldier carries a lance and the other an M-16, the soldier's life remains always the same—the mindset, training, chain of command, fears, risks, mind-numbing routines—soldiers of any era would recognize the warrior in each other instantly if not the weaponry.

Technology comes and goes in a life cycle that repeats through-out history: two steps forward, one or two steps back... The height of one civilization becomes the dark ages of another as technology, the means to produce it, and the knowledge to maintain it, is acquired and lost and acquired once again. Einstein said that he didn't know with what weapons World War III would be fought, but that World War IV would be fought with sticks and stones.

But as all human life and civilization rises and falls and rises again like an enormous, collective respiration, it is our humanity itself that is the constant, the unchanging logic and reason behind humanity's constant change. The predictable cycles of human history are based on the fact that while humanity is always chang-ing, always creating change, humans never do.

Who we are at core, that which makes us human, never changes. Children think their parents have nothing to offer them simply because they don't see themselves reflected in their parents' skin texture, tastes, or lifestyles. But while the differences they see are only skin deep or wholly imagined, the sameness they won't see until later in life goes right to the bone. We look at the record the ancients left us and don't see ourselves reflected in their language, culture, and worldview. But as deep as such cultural distinctions may be, they still lie lightly at the surface, riding the wave of our common humanity, conveying timeless expressions of a deeper and unchanging humanness that remains oblivious to the passage of time.

From parent to child, generation to generation, civilization to civilization, our humanity is passed on unchanged and intact; it must be so or there would be nothing of value, nothing recognizably human in art, literature, or history to glean from one another.

Twenty-eight hundred years ago Homer wrote that when Odysseus returned to his kingdom after twenty years of fighting the Trojans and taking the long way home, the gods held back the dawn to give him and his queen all the time they needed on their first night together again. Who among us doesn't understand such longings and emotion? Who among us hasn't had at least one night we wished would last forever? Even a blind, ancient Greek like Homer can see right into our own souls today and know us better than we know ourselves.

We are alone in our connectedness...

Like someone who can remember only the events of a single day, who wakes each morning from memory-washing sleep as if it were the first day of his or her life, each newborn opens its eyes in utter unknowing as if no other human life had ever been lived. Whatever the little human must learn to become fully ripe must be learned as if for the first time ever—in the single day of a lifetime. The lives of those who went before or come alongside can teach only as well as each learner is willing to accept.

When the student is ready, the teacher will appear. When we are finally ready to see the relevance of every other life to our own, anyone and everyone encountered will begin to teach—and not a moment before. Because even though each one of us begins life tabula rasa, as a blank page and must make our journey alone as if for the first time in human history, there is also a sameness and a connection between every human life that has ever been lived. The sameness lies in that common humanity that makes the shape of our journeys predictable—different in detail, but predictable in shape. The temptation and tendency to see the ancients, or even our own parents, in a different light, a different dispensation, to believe that their journeys were differently shaped by culture or technology, or that God spoke differently to them, is to break the connection between us—to disavow the relevance of anything their lives may have to offer our own.

Like it or not, know it or not, we all live between heaven and earth, between particle and wave, individual and community; we are all alone and all connected, and the quality of our lives is determined by our ability to merge the two—to hold two seemingly disparate elements together in one embrace, to bring heaven to earth and earth to heaven, to see ourselves in each other and each other in ourselves, to love each other *as* ourselves, to walk the Way, to enter Kingdom.

We are alone in finding our connection with each other...

There is a book by Christopher Booker that lays out the case that there are really only seven basic plots to all the stories humans have ever told each other, whether in spoken word, printed word, or film. Joseph Campbell goes even further, saying that there really is only one storyline, the monomyth that we tell ourselves over and over in endless variety. As he puts it in the opening paragraph of *The Hero with a Thousand Faces,*

Whether we listen with aloof amusement to the dreamlike mumbo jumbo of some red-eyed witch doctor of the Congo, or read with cultivated rapture thin translations from the sonnets of the mystic Lao Tzu; now and again, crack the hard nutshell of an argument of Aquinas, or catch suddenly the shining meaning of a bizarre Eskimo fairy tale; it will be always the one, shape-shifting yet marvelously constant story that we find, together with a challengingly persistent suggestion of more remaining to be experienced than will ever be known or told.

At first, such suggestion seems absurd on its face; of course there are more than one or seven stories we tell each other—just look at them all, how different they all are. But more deeply, it's a case of not seeing a forest for the trees. With a step back, the repeating patterns of the forest assert themselves regardless of the variety of individual trees. And why shouldn't they? Our stories—from a wife telling her husband about her day to the epic poems of Homer or Virgil to the plays of Shakespeare or the films of Spielberg and Lucas—are meant to represent some aspect of life and the experience of living it. Our humanity is the common forest in which each of us, as an individual and unique tree, lives out his or her life. A good story, one that accurately represents the experience of living life as a human being, carries with it both the underlying common patterns we all share and the unique details of a specific experience, whether real or imagined.

The archetypal story, the monomyth, outlines the shape of the *hero's journey*: a rite of passage, the spiritual and psychological journey each one of us is called to travel from birth to death and countless times in between. Whoever we are, and whenever we have lived or will live, the shape of the heroic journey is the same for everyone, because God's will, his purpose and desire, is also the same for everyone. The shape of Odysseus' voyage to Troy and back home to Ithaca is the same as Dorothy's voyage to Oz and back to Kansas, which is the same as Luke Skywalker's journey through the Star Wars universe or Frodo's through Middle Earth or Parsifal's quest for the Holy Grail. And the shape of each of these is the same as the shape of the journey each of us will take, as heroes ourselves, if we agree to accept the ride our lives offer.

Campbell tells us there are set stages to the hero's journey, which begins in the ordinary world of everyday life with a call to adventure or action. The hero is called into a strange, new world full of extraordinary and often supernatural characters and events by an imminent threat to the life of his or her community or loved ones, a painful loss or overwhelming desire for something or someone, or by simply stumbling into it, like Alice falling down the rabbit hole. "Your mission should you decide to accept it..." forms the basis of every *Mission: Impossible* and a classic call to action.

In the film version of the *Wizard of Oz*, Dorothy's deep desire for a new life full of color and adventure, along with the threat to her dog's life, leads her to run away from Auntie Em and the colorless farm, putting her on course to meet the exotic Professor Marvel who represents both the world for which she longs and her guide and mentor along the way. Inner restlessness and deep sense of loss, perhaps the loss of her unnamed parents and the home she would have had with them, has spurred in Dorothy the need to find something somewhere out there "over the rainbow."

Once the call to this unusual world has been made, the hero must accept the mission. Sometimes the hero accepts immediately, sometimes refuses repeatedly, delaying the journey. Dorothy tries to refuse the call and end the adventure when the Professor tells her of Auntie Em's distress; she runs back to the farm only to stumble into the twister that takes her to Oz. In her new world, Dorothy as hero must face many difficult trials and tasks in order to complete a journey that she understands only as the need to go "home."

Sometimes the hero must face these trials alone, but often finds the help of a guide or mentor. Dorothy receives help all along her way, from the Professor to a good witch to the Professor again in different roles as doorman, cabbie, the Wizard's guard, and finally as the Wizard himself. She also receives the ruby slippers, a power-ful tool and symbol to wear as she develops strength within herself in the form of Scarecrow, Tin Man, and Lion—her traveling com-panions whose growth along the yellow brick road mirrors her growth within.

The hero's trials climax in severe challenges, which if survived, result in the hero gaining a great gift—a blessing or favor. Dorothy is challenged to bring back the broomstick of the wicked witch, which ushers in her discovery of the identity of the Wizard of Oz and the outpouring of the Wizard's "gifts." As extensions of herself, the gifts her traveling companions receive are really only the insight that Dorothy has received about herself, the discovery of the intelligence, compassion, and courage that had always existed within—and which now lead her to the discovery of the great gift that will define her journey.

The hero then must decide whether to return home to the ordi-nary world, to possibly face more challenges on the return trip, and to bring the blessing of the gift back to the community. Dorothy remains firm in her resolve to return even though parts of her—Scarecrow, Tin Man, and Lion—try to talk her into staying, and Toto sabotages her exit in the Wizard's balloon by diving into the crowd and stranding Dorothy once more.

It is at this moment that Dorothy lets fall all her preconceptions and finally begins to trust the power she has always possessed within and which has always possessed her, the power that animates the ruby slippers. It is a moment of release of everything she had thought her journey was about: as she clicks her heels and wakes up in her bed ringed by all who love her, she sees for the first time the priceless value of everything she has always had in hand and heart. She first thought the journey was about finding new adventure and passion, then she thought it was about finding her way home again; she had to leave to discover what she never had to leave to em-brace...her heart's desire had always been right there, quietly waiting in her own back yard... *If I ever go looking for my heart's desire again, I won't any further than my own back yard. Because if it isn't there, I never really lost it to begin with.*

Her new insight, competence, love, gratitude, and presence are the blessings she brings back to her farm community.

Though many stories and legends don't contain all of these stages—some may have only a few, may focus on just one, or present them in a different order—most include at least the three basic stages of departure/separation, initiation/testing, and return. Why? Why only these basic stages and plotlines for all the stories humans have told each other throughout the ages? It is no coincidence that these three stages—separation, transition, and reincorporation—form the essential elements of a true rite of passage. They mirror and mark the experience of the spiritual/psychological journey that we all must take, both individually and collectively as a people, on our Way to becoming *taba*—the Aramaic word translated as "good," but which from its agrarian roots means ripe, mature, complete. Art must imitate life first before the reverse can ever be true.

We all begin life as the hero begins his or her story, like Adam and Eve in the Garden: infants at home, not knowing we're naked, at peace and content with life. But through a wounding or loss or threat, paradise is lost, and we are called to begin a search to regain our contentment, our bliss, which may have been lost for so long we can barely remember ever having had it or may even assume we're searching to find it for the very first time.

This call comes early in life, too early for some as the cover of childhood is pulled by neglect, abuse, or some form of trauma. For others, the angst and restlessness of adolescence are the physical, psychological, and spiritual manifestations of the call to leave the too-small Garden of the child and enter the too-large, terrifying world of the adult. For many or most of us, that new world is just too big, too frightening and unfamiliar to immediately enter, and the call is refused. But to refuse the call, to retreat back to the Garden of our childhood only to find it locked and guarded by angels with flaming swords, to camp outside it—unable to go back, afraid to go forward—is to negate the very purpose and desire of God to be ripening always toward perfect unity with him and each other. From Joseph Campbell again:

> Often in actual life, and not infrequently in the myths and popular tales, we encounter the dull case of the call unanswered; for it is always possible to turn the ear to other interests. Refusal of the summons converts the adventure into its negative. Walled in boredom, hard work, or "culture," the subject loses the power of significant affirmative action and becomes a victim to be saved. His flowering world becomes a wasteland of dry stones and his life feels meaningless...
>
> "Because I have called and you refused...I also will laugh at your calamity; I will mock when your fear comes; when your fear comes as desolations, and your destruction comes as a whirlwind; when distress and anguish come upon you." (Proverbs 1:24-27)

No longer children, but not yet willing to be adults, looking to the outside world as ripe and ready, but hard and green inside, there is not much point to a life like this. Yeshua curses the fig tree in Matthew 21 that looks from a distance to be ripe and full of fruit, but on closer inspection contains no more than leaves and branches; his "curse" is to expose its inability to nourish life, its inner withered nature.

If the call is not answered in the angst of adolescence, the energy and momentum of youth typically propel us through our twenties to the angst of the mid-life crisis of either our thirties or forties. If the call is still refused, the caricature of the mid-life crisis can manifest with all the material trappings of remembered youth—cars, clothing, promiscuity—being sought with a vengeance. If we are too fearful to go forward and accept our mission in the strange new world, at some point we subconsciously throw ourselves bodily back against the gates of the familiar old world of our youth. If we can't come to believe that love and security can exist in the harsh world of the adult, we attempt to crawl back to the arms or womb of infancy and childhood, trying to regain the contentment we subconsciously recall.

Tragically, many of us remain in this hell until the pain and self-destruction we inflict on ourselves and others become so great, they eclipse even our fear, and in that moment we may also find a kind of release in having nothing left to lose, possibly regaining the ability to move forward again for the first time since childhood. But at what cost comes such passive release from the unanswered call?

The call to engage the hero's journey is always a call to authentic spirituality but not necessarily a call to religion. The journey may well include religious experience, but the call is to an inward search for meaning that ultimately can't be found in the world outside—even though full engagement in the tasks of that world is how we answer. Ultimately, the hero's journey is not the journey itself, but a repeated looking beneath the surface activity, finding the *tasks within the tasks* that carry lasting meaning and show us who we really are. Without awareness of that deeper significance, we are choosing to fiercely identify with exterior roles, tasks, and accomplishments in order to survive the nothingness of the felt loss of deepest purpose. What are all the addictions, compulsions, and dysfunctional relationships in which we engage, the "sins" of the distraction and division we create, but attempts to drown out God's persistent, unflagging call to himself?

When the call to heroic adventure is accepted at whatever stage in life, through the twists and turns of our journey far from home, we begin to learn the truth about ourselves, life, deepest purpose, and the relationship between them. We gather the gifts and tools we find along the way that assist and guide us through the trials we face until we reach the climax, the moment of release that ultimately defines our journey.

This release is conveyed by Yeshua with two Aramaic words related in meaning. *Subqana*, the Aramaic word translated as both "release" and "forgiveness" in Luke 4:18 as Yeshua stands in the synagogue at Nazareth reading from Isaiah 61, means release, liberation, forgiveness, being restored or allowed to return to an original state. But the release of *subqana* is always based on the knowing of *sherara*—translated as "truth" in John 8:32 and also as "set free" at Luke 4:18. Its roots include that which liberates, is strong and vigorous, and opens new possibilities to right and harmonious directions. Translating Luke 4:18 directly from the Aramaic, Yeshua is saying his mission is to set free, *sherara*, with forgiveness, *subqana*, those who are oppressed.

To *set free with forgiveness* is an odd phrase to our ears until we consider how forgiveness can liberate. The release of forgiveness, the return to the awareness of connection with which we were born and lost along the way, is the truth, the new possibility that makes us free enough, fearless enough to pursue our true purpose and identity apart from the mere tasks we initially set out to accomplish.

We can then return with these blessings to the Garden from which we began—but not the too-small Garden of unknowing childhood, but the conscious Garden of mature contentment that we now know has always existed within, in our own back yards, and will now give us the power to bless others in our community.

The moment of release goes by many names.

Sometimes it is called enlightenment, brightening, or illumination. Yeshua called it being reborn, drinking living water, or eating the bread of life; Paul called it transformation; the New Testament collectively calls it salvation, which the Hebrews understood as spiritual release or liberation right herenow. Philosopher Immanuel Kant famously wrote that "Enlightenment is man's release from self-imposed immaturity and dependence for which he himself was responsible." Shakespeare more famously wrote that a rose by any other name would smell as sweet...

From a Hebrew perspective, Yeshua is saying that release from everything we mistakenly thought our lives and our journeys were about, the substitution of truth for illusion, and the realization of the true love-nature of God is all the salvation we can ever expect or will ever need.

○ ◑ ◐ ⊕ ⊘

In another hero's journey, this time from a film called *Hero*, a nameless warrior of ancient China sets out to assassinate the king of a competing kingdom who has ravaged his homeland. Nameless is devastated by loss and motivated by revenge. He sees his mission as the eradication of the evil that created his wounding and that of his community. But in order to reach the king and accomplish the task he has set for himself, he must first overcome another warrior, Broken Sword, who had also initially set out to assassinate the king, but met his moment of release instead.

In preparation for his assault on the king, Broken Sword sought to perfect his swordsmanship by immersing himself in the art of calligraphy, understanding the kinship between brush and sword. But the mastery of his art sets him on an inward journey of which he himself was not fully aware until he finally comes face to face with the king. At the moment he is free to strike and complete his mission, he sees the king's true heart and the path to the greatest good, and does not kill him.

Realizing that Nameless can't be defeated by the sword or forcefully stopped in his quest for revenge against the king, Broken Sword presents him with two calligraphies to consider. As Nameless struggles to understand the symbols he has been given, he begins his own journey to interior places far beneath the anguish and desire for revenge that animate his self-appointed task.

The first symbol translates as "all under heaven" or "our land" from a Chinese proverb: "To suffer yourself when all under heaven suffer, to enjoy only when all under heaven enjoy." This expression of the unity of all things teaches Nameless that every action must be motivated by the needs of all under heaven, that he is inextricably linked to everyone around him and can't help but suffer when they suffer and can only enjoy his life to the extent that all others do as well. His narrow view of the righteousness of a two-dimensional quest for revenge, the removal of the power that threatens his community, must be merged or even submerged into the quest for the greatest good for all under heaven, regardless of his personal desires.

The second calligraphy, deciphered only in the last frames of the film as Nameless prepares to strike the king, delivers a statement of the threeness of mastery in the martial arts: "Unity of man and sword" is the first stage, where anything, even a blade of grass can become a weapon—ultimate mastery in which there is no longer any distinction between man and sword; they are one. The second: "The sword exists in one's heart," where physical practice has become so spiritually internalized that entire battles can be fought completely within the locked gaze of poised warriors: the fight stopped, won or lost, before it is ever begun. And finally, "The absence of sword in hand or heart," where weapons and even the need for battle itself are discarded as the warrior finds identity and oneness, not with his art or weapon, but with all under heaven.

Nameless, like Broken Sword before him, travels a hero's journey to his moment of the release of everything he thought his life and mission were about. He too sees the true heart of the king and his role in the events of history, laying down his own life for the good of all under heaven.

When God calls Abram to set out on a journey "to the land which I will show you," it is with the promise that his family will be made into a great nation, a blessed nation through whom "all the families of the earth will be blessed." For Abram, now called Abraham, this promise of the immortality of his lineage flows through the veins of his son, the miracle child, Isaac, born when he and his wife were over a hundred years old. Though the impossible birth of Isaac had seemed to cement the reality of an equally impossible promise, that promise was only realized at Abraham's moment of release, the climax of his journey when he realizes that God's promise has nothing to do with flesh and blood descendants. When he becomes willing to release everything he thought was true by being willing to sacrifice his son, the very vehicle through whom he believed all promise was to pass, Abraham becomes the father of a nation he couldn't have imagined. Abraham had thought that Isaac was the agent of God's will—turns out it was his own faith instead. It is the laying aside of his limited expectation, the laying down of his desired outcome for the good of all under heaven that lays the foundation of faith that is the true fulfillment of the promise. Abraham's faith is the gift he finds along the Way, his immortal legacy, and humanity's blessing. The journey is completed, the mission accomplished, but in a way never contemplated by Abraham until that moment.

Many generations later, Moses is called to journey from his exile in Midian back to Egypt, to the Pharaoh himself. Moses believes he is engaging a mission to free his people from bondage and lead them to a land promised by God, "to a good and spacious land, to a land flowing with milk and honey." After forty years wandering in the wilderness, at the summit of Mount Nebo, Moses sees the Promised Land stretching out to the shores of the western sea. But at this, the climax of his journey, he realizes he will never enter. At his moment of release, Moses understands that the Promised Land is not the real estate rolled out before him, but the Kingdom of

Heaven itself—the promised life of a nation living in the awareness and presence of their God. In this land, a Moses has no place. As prophet and wayshower, the only man to whom God spoke, Moses is a venerated distraction, a man to whom the people will turn instead of personally engaging the journey themselves. At this moment, Moses willingly lays down his life for the good of all under heaven.

Many generations later, a young Solomon is called by God in a dream to ask for that which he most desires as he sets off on his journey as king. Solomon asks for wisdom, which God willingly grants, and wisdom becomes the object of Solomon's lifelong quest as king. It is only at the climax of his long journey, as his own death draws near, that Solomon reaches his moment of release—the moment in which he realizes that everything he had sought and everything he had accomplished had nothing to do with the end he so desired. It wasn't wisdom itself that mattered; wisdom was just another word for vanity, futility, and striving after the wind. But after a lifetime of practicing wisdom, Solomon finally becomes wise. In the release of having nothing left to lose, in the final betrayal of all he had labored to produce, he finds a truth that makes him free, a contentment rooted only in simple presence to daily life, but far deeper than anything he could accomplish with his hands or think with his mind, and he lays down his life's work for the good of all under heaven.

As with all these great heroes, when we answer our own calls and set off, the journey is never what we think it is. The issue at hand is never the real issue, because the physical tasks to which we set ourselves can only find completion externally in our roles and accomplishments, firmly staking our sense of identity, meaning, and purpose somewhere over the rainbow. Whether we set off in life to build a business or a legacy or even to feed the hungry or save souls for God, our true purpose is not the completion of any of these. But if we are true to the physical task, in the course of facing the inevitable trials along the way, we begin to learn about life, to see relationship where we previously saw only separation, to draw connections between dots that seemed previously unconnected. Almost in spite of ourselves and regardless of our stated task, if we persist long enough, we will stumble across the trailhead to Yeshua's Way, fall down the rabbit hole, and if we're willing, let the real interior journey begin.

A hero is not someone who sets out and successfully completes the task he or she expected to accomplish. A hero is someone who simply sets out...and in the setting out, accomplishes the unexpected. A hero allows himself to be blown off course; allows herself to be gathered up into the eye of the whirlwind; patiently shrugs off repeated shovels of dirt dropped into the well of preconception; releases everything believed to be crucial at the outset of the journey in favor of what really is. A hero engages fully, holds nothing back, becomes willing to lay down the mission itself when a greater good presents, and becomes ultimately willing to lay down his or her own life for the good of all under heaven. A hero allows the journey to unfold at its own pace, relishing the surprise and shock of unanticipated vistas—allows the mission to be accomplished in ways never dreamed, continuing on until the circle is complete, until he or she is home again with blessing in hand for all under heaven. Recalling T.S. Eliot: "And the end of all our exploring will be to arrive where we started and know the place for the first time."

> A hero is not the one who completes the journey,
> but the one whom the journey completes.

Many of us who set off on our spiritual hero's journey become mired along the way because we stop too soon—before we reach *twelveness*, the sacred number of the completed cycle from January to December and back to January, the perfection of the material earth and earthly governance, the arrival of the New Jerusalem. Ultimately unwilling to release what we think we know about the journey, no matter how hard we've worked or how much we've accomplished, we remain unreleased. We continue to confuse external tasks and challenges, religion, spiritual technique or practice with the journey itself, and though we may have changed uniforms, professions, or churches, who we think we are hasn't changed at all.

As in the three-stage journey of the martial artist, "unity of man and sword" is only the first step, yet we treat it as both first and last, working so hard to master the elements of our faith—our practices, our theology, the text of our Scriptures (we even call the Bible our "sword")—that when we feel we have that sword firmly in hand, our religion and religious texts mastered, we believe we have fully and finally arrived. As masters of the sword of the Word, we cling to it in obedience and wield it as any sword is wielded, creating battles, division, and separation wherever we direct our efforts.

Ironically, in all our mastery of Scripture, we have drowned out God's voice calling us in those same Scriptures to "impress these words of mine on your heart and on your soul," (Deuteronomy 11:18) urging us on to the second stage where "the sword exists in one's heart," where ideas and concepts become action—a way of living life in which we "think" in God's native language without the need for translation, and where battles and divisions are stopped before they begin in the locked gaze of a people steeped in the unity of love—not the mastery of technique.

And even beyond this, Yeshua's enigmatic saying, "For whoever wishes to save his life will lose it; but whoever loses his life for my sake will find it," is nothing less than the call to step completely out of ourselves, out of who and what we think we are, to continue on until we find "the absence of sword in hand or heart:" where even the need for a sword or a battle falls away, where training wheels are removed, Law is fulfilled and obviated, *mamlacha* graduates to *malkuth*, and we can say with Serapion, "I have sold the book which told me to sell all that I had and give to the poor."

Standing naked again in the Garden, as contented and unarmed as the day we began—our very shed skin lying dry and empty at our feet: post-theology, post-religion, post-law, post-practice, post-thought, even post-mortem—is the completion of the hero's journey, the completion of the hero, the twelveness of the Way. But even then, one cycle is not the end any more than one cycle could fully define the infinite. Our heroic, called-out lives trace an infinite cycle of cycles just large enough to keep the eternal present moment filled right to the brim at any moment we choose to fall in.

ⵘ ⵘ ⵘ ⵘ ⵘ

Just as all this may seem to be too much, beyond the strength of mere mortals, Yeshua appears again with a broad smile on his face and a pair of ruby slippers in his hands. The smile reminds us of the manner in which we are loved and how much fun this all should really be, and the slippers remind us that...

> It's not as difficult as we think.
> Ultimately, it's *only* as difficult as we think.

Ever the master of brevity, Yeshua's call to us, his encouragement and the slippers he would place on our feet as we set out along the Way, comes as a *threeness*, another completed cycle—three words: ask, seek, and knock... "Ask, and it will be given to you; seek, and you will find; knock, and it will be opened to you. For everyone who asks receives, and he who seeks finds, and to him who knocks it will be opened." (Matthew 7)

As always, it is in Yeshua's native language that we find deepest meaning to his promise. Ask, *selu* in Aramaic, is not a polite, passive request, but more like a police interrogation, an intense questioning with a sense of urgency, carrying the intensity of begging, craving, desiring, or requiring. As a form of *sela*, Aramaic for prayer, *selu* includes the root meanings of inclining toward, leaning into, lying in wait, and paints the picture of intense desire, a craving for something we can't give ourselves that causes us to clear a space in our lives and look expectantly for its arrival. For Yeshua, to ask is to desire deeply enough to take action.

Seek, *be'a*, to search diligently from inside to outside, is no casual looking, but again an intense endeavoring, enquiring, requiring. *Be'a* is *selu* in action, an intense, driven, passionate search from the inside to the outside of our lives, the commitment to leave no stone unturned in order to satisfy our desire and craving for truth.

Finally to knock, *qoshw*, surprisingly means to pitch or strike as one would pitch a tent or strike a musical note. Sharing roots with *qadash*, which means holy, *qoshw* can be understood as a setting apart for specific purpose, a clearing or sweeping or hollowing out of a special place. To knock is the careful, patient, diligent preparation of a special place in our lives for God's presence to become real. It is the opening up to the reality of that presence.

There is nothing at all passive about asking, seeking, and knocking in Yeshua's meaning. For the promise of the giving, finding, and opening to be realized, we must actively extend and expend ourselves along the Way. But even as Yeshua places these slippers on our feet, he is telling us that the power to animate them already exists within us, that there is nothing to find "out there" that can take us home. The journey along the Way to Kingdom is always traveled from inside out, within confines of our own backyards and like destiny and God's will, is not a "what" at all, but simply a "how." It's not about discovering deep theological truths or building great cathedrals for God; it's always and only about enjoying the ride—while we discover deep truths and build whatever we build—a falling in love with each and every person and relationship and created thing that we find along the Way.

When we fall in love with the Way and everyone and everything on it, when we suddenly find ourselves playing along the Way instead of working our way through, we have reached our moment of release and received the gifts God is presenting: we have simultaneously entered Kingdom, found God's will, and met our destiny. All that remains is to return home, that is, to re-turn to face the nearest person, our neighbor, and share the gift of our presence, a presence now filled with God's presence, purpose, and deepest desire. With these gifts in hand, all creation is blessed—able to be enjoyed, partaken, by all under heaven.

To really understand Yeshua's message and Way is to realize that he too is only telling one story, transmitting one message over and over in as many different settings and with as many different faces as possible.

The Kingdom of Heaven is like...

...a gardener, scattered seed, leaven in a bag of flour, a treasure in a field, a merchant seeking fine pearls, a fishing net cast upon the sea, the head of a household, a king settling accounts, a landowner hiring laborers, a wedding feast, a mustard seed which becomes a great tree, young girls tending their lamps, being born again, a Roman centurion, a Samaritan, a father with a rebellious son, a child playing in the street...

It's the same, shape-shifting story of Kingdom that he always tells, the same, solitary message of the Way that he always desires to impress—that this Way was not traveled by him *for* us, in our place, but was traveled as Wayshower, as encouragement for us to scamper after. It is not an impossible journey or beyond the reach of any of us—it's not any more difficult than we believe it to be and can be borne on the backs of the least of us—actually is borne best by the least of us.

The Way is not a journey to be endured, but to be enjoyed,
and in the most real sense, until we *are* enjoying it,
the journey has really not even begun.

The truth that makes us free, the truth of our release is always hiding in plain sight; there is no mystery, no esoteric knowledge to gain, nothing that is not immediately apparent to a child's eye. We need no special skills or preparation or intermediaries to set a course and go; our journey begins with desire alone and is sustained by desire alone—God's own desire, his *sebyana*—which leads always homeward to the pitched tent of God's presence.

When all else has failed, when we have no idea where we are going and no longer see the road ahead and feel we've completely lost our Way, it's our desire alone that is sufficient, that pleases God and whisks us back into his presence at the click of our heels.

And with each breathless homecoming, as the Father is sprinting up to drape himself around the neck of another returning son or daughter, as each bedraggled hero adds another story to the story of all humanity, the realization grows that every homecoming, every individual moment of release is one more golden brick in the twelveness, the eventual and inevitable completion of the New *Yerushalayim*...the release of all under heaven.

CHALLENGE
*Life's challenges and accomplishments have no meaning of their own;
released from that illusion, we find the deeper meaning with which we began.*

WALKABOUT

ENGAGING THE WAY

Cruel, Crazy, Beautiful World

You must live in the present, launch yourself on every wave,
find your eternity in each moment. Fools stand on their
island of opportunities and look toward another land.
There is no other land; there is no other life but this.

Henry David Thoreau

WHEN I WAS AROUND NINE OR TEN YEARS OLD, I GOT A CHEMISTRY
set for my birthday or Christmas or some such occasion. I don't
remember the reason, but I do remember the chemistry set. I
remember that I thought it was beautiful. Way back then in the
mid-sixties, things were still made mostly of metal; plastics were on
the way, but hadn't fully arrived. So in my bedroom with the door
shut, I had all the time in the world to pore over the metal case
about two feet high and foot and a half wide. It was all brightly
painted with a clasp on one side and opened up like a book to
expose two full panels of shelving containing test tubes and racks,
pipettes and vials and rubber tubing, and dozens of sealed bottles
of neatly labeled chemicals.

I would sit there and look at all the equipment, pull it out, and
set it up. I'd open each bottle of chemical compounds and smell it,
shake it, then reseal it and put it back. I'd look through the book
that came with the set and read about the possible experiments,
then put the equipment back on the little shelves exactly as it had

come shipped in the box. Those experiments involved water and mixing and using up the precious chemicals; they were messy affairs, after which the beautiful case would never be the same—the shiny racks and tubes would never look the same. I remember that chemistry set well, but I don't have a single memory of even one experiment conducted with it.

A few years later when I was playing high school football, I found myself largely on the bench during the games. Those of us who routinely rode the bench quickly learned that one of the most humiliating experiences in our short sports careers was to run off the field at the end of the game, past all of the students and parents in the stands, with a uniform so brightly white-clean that everyone knew at a glance we'd never gotten out of a sitting position all night. It was as if we glowed in the dark running next to the sweaty, filthy starters. But there is a certain amount of anonymity that a football helmet gives you, and people's attention spans being what they are, as long as you had some amount of green and brown streaks on your pants, you got the benefit of the doubt.

So those of us not certain whether we'd play that night, would work hard to get as dirty as possible during the pre-game warm ups and exercises to ensure a little respect, no matter how dubious, during the post-game race for the lockers.

> You can't play the game without getting your uniform dirty. And if your uniform isn't dirty, everyone knows you didn't play the game.

In the six years it took me to get from fourth to tenth grade, I'd learned to value something dirty over something clean; something well used over something pristine. Thank God... I wasted that chemistry set by never using it, and though I may have also wasted my time playing football, the experience taught me something critically unrelated to the game—*a task within the task*: that uniforms are made to get dirty, that chemicals are neatly bottled to be used in messy experiments. That our lives have been given to us to expend fully; our bodies, so smooth and taut in the beginning, are made to be worn out over a lifetime of the trial and error of messy relationship.

It is no different in the spiritual realm. Whatever we think we know or understand about God and life is wasted if we don't pour it all out into the lives of the people around us and see what happens. It's a great experiment of sorts: we can theorize and theologize all we want, but we'll never know if what we say we believe is true, is true enough to make us free from our fears, until we use it all up in the mess of seeing for ourselves. I was afraid if I used all my chemicals, I wouldn't be able to get more, so I used none at all. But God always has another bottle of whatever I need in his pocket; I can use all I want with abandon.

And so we are at the point where we need to get out of the classroom and into the street. We need to take those chemicals and those uniforms and use them all up and get really dirty in the process.

It's all rubber and road stuff from here on out: what does it matter if we can define the hypostatic union of Christ's divine and human natures if we can't balance our marriages or our check books? What good are our beliefs about God if they don't make our lives and relationships sing out loud right herenow? We live at the level of life—sweaty, bloody, beautiful life. If our spirituality can't withstand the intensity of that life, if it can't endure and thrive there, then what good is it? It's not true enough, and it's not saving or liberating enough either.

◌ ◍ ◎ ⊕ ⊘

This is what life is like. And anything not like this is not living.

Our lives, if lived well, are marked with rites of passage, but life, however lived, *is* a rite of passage. We are separated at conception or shortly thereafter from something or someone we can't see or smell but suspect is somewhere, just there, over our rainbows... Our entire lives are a transition to the re-incorporation of death, the reconnection of everything to everywhen: everything experienced all at once instead of strung out along imaginary timelines. To begin to see life this way—wheels within wheels—always cycling back to the timeless time from which we came and *always* are, except in our minds, is the very beginning of our enjoyment of it.

There is only one Way to the Father, to the wholeness and completion of re-incorporation. It's a messy, risky, painful, immersive, exhilarating affair that Johnny Clegg called a cruel, crazy, beautiful world. That's it, exactly. Contradiction and paradox alongside beauty and order. Harmony alongside discord, kindness alongside inconceivable cruelty.

The secret to life is learning to love that there is no answer to life, no resolving the adventure of simply not knowing.

We either live it or we don't. No one is exempt.

Yeshua's life story as preserved in the gospels is a perfectly framed hero's journey. Not exempt himself from the cycle of separation, transition, and re-incorporation, Yeshua *is* the cycle, the Way, the course of life that Carl Jung called an "almost perfect map" of human transformation. Yeshua's walkabout, his essential rite of passage, drove him through the wilderness of his temptation for forty days and forty nights just as Noah before him endured forty days in the rain and Moses forty days on the summit of Sinai and forty years leading his people through waterless places.

Knit deeply into the psyche of Semitic people, the number forty symbolized a time of trial and initiation into rebirth—a rite of passage, of course—and Yeshua's eighteen unaccounted years in the gospels imply a much longer walkabout, a much longer transition in which Yeshua was pushed to the breaking point.

Facing down the three temptations of the adversary or accuser—as the Aramaic words would directly translate—Yeshua presents us with another symbolic number. The Semitic *threeness* of completion and perfection points to the universality of Yeshua's trials, the sum of all human need that Henri Nouwen so perfectly described as the need to be relevant, powerful, and spectacular—that Richard Rohr lists as our most basic emotional programs...the need for survival and security, power and control, affection and esteem. Looked at this way, the adversary's temptations to turn stones into bread, gain dominion over the kingdoms of the earth, and to be carried by angels in sight of an adoring crowd rise off the printed page to morph into the blur of compulsive choices we make each and every day of our lives. Yeshua's innate human needs and compulsions are no different than ours, and the passage through them has not changed in all of human history.

On his walkabout through the wilderness, even when he was at the end of himself, Yeshua was never alone. He carried within himself the collective wisdom of his people—a hundred generations walking with him—as sure a guide through the bush as any songline sung by an uncertain aboriginal boy. Yeshua's guide through the wilderness of compulsive human need, his songlines, were the stories, poetry, and prophecy contained in the writings of his people—meticulously copied and handed down, connecting each generation to every generation and tracing the shape of their journey through the land with each other and their God. From creation to Kingdom, these songs, rehearsed daily upon rising up and lying down and everywhen in between moved beyond mere memory to become a part of his being, and his entire being became the map to the passage of his life.

At every point of contact with the adversary, at every exhausting challenge, Yeshua sings songs from the books of his people and threads his way to freedom: *it is written, man shall not live by bread alone; you shall worship the Lord your God and serve him only; you shall not put the Lord your God to the test.* Yeshua had become the book, the songs that follow the shape of the wilderness, leading him back to the Galilee, his home and his people. But not the same Yeshua.

Just as Moses returned from the mountain with his hair whitened by the experience of God's presence, the people are amazed at Ye-shua: isn't this the carpenter, Mary's son, they ask. Isn't he the brother of James, Joses, Judas, and Simon? Aren't his sisters with us? (Mark 6) They are amazed and offended, but no one can deny the authority of his teaching, the gentleness of his manner, or the bril-liance of his smile. Children flock to him while the powerful carefully watch. Whether they liked it or not, believed it or not, celebrated or not...and however or whenever we now believe the miracle to have occurred...

...Yeshua and the Father were one.

Written songlines had taken Yeshua on a journey that couldn't be contained on a written page. Navigating the songs of his people, Yeshua, like the prophets before him, began singing new songs—as yet unwritten—that he heard his Father singing over landscapes stitched together by the music of his passage. And upon his return, singing those new songs to his people, those with ears to hear began to see the shape of new lands in their midst calling them to be the heroes of their own journeys, to make passages that would bring them back where they started, but not the same people: transformed people, whitened and convinced of what they were convinced of.

Yeshua's new songs, improvised with his Father over the written songs of a hundred generations have now been passed on to us as the written songs of another hundred generations. But these songs are also just marks scratched on paper. There is no music until we sing them, *become* them with countless renditions, immerse until the moment of our passage arrives, and we embark on a journey of our own in which *we* will hear our Father singing new songs as yet unwritten...variations on ancient themes that will become the songs of our own conviction.

Yeshua created a Calvary moment for himself long before the Romans did. By leaving all the familiar sounds and relationships of home for the silent sterility of the wilderness, he met the death of his distractions, just as Spirit had impelled him to do. For Yeshua, it was an extreme exterior journey that cleared the way for an interior truth: recognition of his true identity, meaning, and purpose. And like the rich young man, when we ask this Yeshua what we must do to obtain eternal life, and he sees the sincerity of our desire, are we ready to hear his unexpected answer?

When we sincerely ask, we only hear truth. Whether we're ready to listen for such new possibility is what we will learn from our own reactions. Yeshua answers with the only way to the Father, a way not made of words, but the shape of Calvary, the death of the distractions that keep us from seeing our Father right herenow and knowing the nature of our own identity, meaning, and purpose. Do we need to leave home, job, and family and immerse in a physical wilderness to follow his Way?

Following Yeshua is not a *what* but a *how*; the details of his exterior journey are his, not ours. The details of our exterior journey will be of our own choosing, but will always include the primal elements of silence, solitude, prayer, meditation, community, and service that build in us the interior elements of humility, gratitude, and stillness from which truth can no longer hide.

And if the songs we sing upon our return to the ring of faces we have known and loved our entire lives bear the marks of our passage and our conviction, our people will see the change in us, be amazed, possibly offended, but never unmoved.

This is the Way of it. Jesus' original challenge. There is no other.

It's time to relearn the songlines that connect all the generations of our people to our land and our God. It's time to go walkabout, led by the map of our collected wisdom and the ears to hear our Father's voice singing new songs that will take us places we will add to the music of generations after for the good of all under heaven.

It's time to move out into the country, get some fresh air.

Selected Sources and Additional Reading

HEBREW/ARAMAIC LANGUAGE, CULTURE, WORLDVIEW

Benner, Jeff. *His Name is One: An Ancient Hebrew Perspective of the Name of God.* VirtualBookWorm, 2003.

Bivin, David, and Roy B. Blizzard. *Understanding the Difficult Words of Jesus.* Treasure House, 1994.

Borman, Thorleif. *Hebrew Thought Compared with Greek.* W.W. Norton & Company, 2002.

Bruce, F.F. *Hard Sayings of Jesus.* InterVarsity Press, 1983.

Douglas-Klotz, Neil. *The Hidden Gospel: Decoding the Spiritual Message of the Aramaic Jesus.* Quest Books, 2001.

Douglas-Klotz, Neil. *Prayers of the Cosmos: Meditations on the Aramaic Words of Jesus.* HarperSanFrancisco, 1993.

Friedman, David. *They Loved the Torah: What Yeshua's First Followers Really Thought About the Law.* Messianic Jewish Resources International, 2001.

Moseley, Ron. Yeshua: *A Guide to the Real Jesus and the Original Church.* Messianic Jewish Resources International, 1998.

Munk, Michael. *The Wisdom in the Hebrew Alphabet.* Artscroll, 1986.

Stern, David H. *Restoring the Jewishness of the Gospel: A Message for Christians.* Jewish New Testament Publications, Inc., 1988.

Wilson, Marvin. *Our Father Abraham: Jewish Roots of the Christian Faith.* Wm B. Eerdsmans Publishing Company, 1989.

Young, Brad. *Jesus the Jewish Theologian.* Hendrickson Publishers, 1995.

LEXICONS AND GRAMMARS

Benner, Jeff. *The Ancient Hebrew Language and Alphabet: Understanding the Ancient Hebrew Language of the Bible Based on the Ancient Hebrew Culture and Thought.* VirtualBookWorm, 2004.

Benner, Jeff. *Ancient Hebrew Lexicon of the Bible: Hebrew Letters, Words and Roots Defined Within Their Ancient Cultural Context.* VirtualBookWorm, 2005.

Kaufman, Steven, ed. *Comprehensive Aramaic Lexicon.* Hebrew Union College, cal1.cn.huc.edu.

Jennings, William. *Lexicon to the Syriac New Testament.* Oxford at the Clarendon Press, 1926.

Smith, J. Payne. *A Compendious Syriac Dictionary.* Wipf and Stock Publishers, 1999.

Aramaic Lexicon and Concordance. The Way International, 1989. Aramaicpeshitta.com.

English Dictionary Supplement to the Concordance to the Peshitta Version of the Aramaic New Testament. American Christian Press, 1985.

The Concordance to the Peshitta Version of the Aramaic New Testament. American Christian Press, 1985.

Strong, James. *Strong's Exhaustive Concordance of the Bible.* Hendrickson Publishers, 2007.

BIBLE TRANSLATIONS AND COMMENTARIES

Barnes, Albert. *Barnes Notes on the Old and New Testaments.* Baker Books, 1983.

Clarke, Adam. *Commentary on the Entire Bible.* Baker Book House, 1971.

Daniel, Orville. *A Harmony of the Four Gospels.* Baker Books, 1996.

Gill, John. *Exposition of the Old and New Testaments.* Baptist Standard Bearer, 2006.

Jamieson, R. *Jamieson, Fausset and Brown Commentary on the Whole Bible.* Zondervan, 1999.

Lamsa, George M. *Holy Bible from the Ancient Eastern Text.* Harper Collins, 1968.

Peterson, Eugene H. *The Message.* Navpress, 1988.

Stern, David. *Complete Jewish Bible.* Jewish New Testament Publications, 1998.

Stern, David. *Jewish New Testament.* Messianic Jewish Resources International, 1989.

Stern, David. *Jewish New Testament Commentary.* Messianic Jewish Resources International, 1992.

Younan, Paul. *Aramaic/English Peshitta Interlinear New Testament.* Peshitta.org, 2000.

Eight Translation New Testament. Tyndale House Publishers, 1974.

Vincent, Marvin. *Vincent's Word Studies in the New Testament.* Hendrickson Publishers, 1985.

ORIGIN OF SCRIPTURE/CHRISTIANITY, CHURCH HISTORY

Barnstone, Willis, Ed. *The Other Bible.* Harper & Row, 1983

Cairns, Earle E. *Christianity through the Centuries.* Academie Books, 1981.

Cameron, Ron, ed. *The Other Gospels.* The Westminster Press, 1982.

Mack, Burton L. *Who Wrote the New Testament?* Harper Collins, 1995.

Mack, Burton L. *The Lost Gospel: The Book of Q and Christian Origins.* Harper Collins, 1994.

Maier, Paul, L. *Josephus, The Essential Writings: A Condensation of Jewish Antiquities and the Jewish War.* Kregel Publications, 1988.

Mead, Frank S. *Handbook of Denominations in the United States.* Abingdon Press, 1995.

Miller, Robert J., Ed. *The Complete Gospels.* Polebridge Press, 1992.

Pagels, Elaine. *The Gnostic Gospels.* Vintage Books, 1979.

Sailhamer, John H. *How We Got the Bible.* Zondervan Publishing House, 1998.

Wegner, Paul D. *The Journey from Text to Translation: The Origin and Development of the Bible.* Baker Academic, 1999

Vermes, G. *The Dead Sea Scrolls in English.* Pelican Books, 1962.

Zondervan Handbook to the Bible. Zondervan Publishing House, 1999.

CHRISTIAN SPIRITUALITY

Manning, Brennan. *The Ragamuffin Gospel: Good News for the Bedraggled, Beat-Up, and Burnt-Out.* Multnomah, 2000.

Manning, Brennan. *Ruthless Trust: The Ragamuffin's Path to God.* HarperSanFrancisco, 2002.

Manning, Brennan. *Abba's Child: The Cry of the Heart for Intimate Belonging.* Navpress Publishing Group, 2002.

Nouwen, Henri. *Life of the Beloved: Spiritual Living in a Secular World.* Crossroads General Interest, 2002.

Nouwen, Henri. *Return of the Prodigal Son: A Story of Homecoming.* Image, 1994.

Nouwen, Henri. *The Way of the Heart: Desert Spirituality and Contemporary Ministry.* HarperSanFrancisco, 1991.

Nouwen, Henri. *Out of Solitude: Three Meditations on the Christian Life.* Ave Maria Press, 2004

Yancey, Philip. *What's So Amazing About Grace?* Zondervan, 2002.

CONTEMPLATIVE PRAYER, SPIRITUAL JOURNEY

Anonymous. *The Cloud of Unknowing.* HarperSanFrancisco, 2004.

Bochen, Christine M., ed. *Thomas Merton: Essential Writings.* Orbis Books, 2000.

Brother Lawrence. *The Practice of the Presence of God.* Whitaker House, 1982.

Cunningham, Lawrence S., ed. *Thomas Merton: Spiritual Master.* Paulist Press, 1992.

Keating, Thomas. *Invitation to Love: The Way of Christian Contemplation.* Continuum International Publishing Group, 1994

Keating, Thomas. *Open Mind, Open Heart: The Contemplative Dimension of the Gospel.* Continuum International Publishing Group, 1994

Merton, Thomas. *The Seven Storey Mountain.* Harcourt, 1999.

Merton, Thomas. *The New Seeds of Contemplation.* New Directions Publishing Corp., 1972.

Merton, Thomas. *The Wisdom of the Desert: Sayings from the Desert Fathers of the Fourth Century.* Shambhala, 2004.

Merton, Thomas. *Thoughts in Solitude.* Farrar, Straus and Giroux, 1999.

THEOLOGICAL ISSUES

Enns, Paul. *The Moody Handbook of Theology.* Moody Press, 1989.

Instone-Brewer, David. *Divorce and Remarriage in the Bible: The Social and Literary Context.* Wm. B. Eerdsmans Publishing Company, 2002.

Lewis, C.S. *The Great Divorce.* Fount, 2002.

Lewis, C.S. *The Problem of Pain.* HarperSanFrancisco, 2001.

Merton, Thomas. *Opening the Bible.* Fortress Press/The Liturgical Press, 1970.

Virkler, Henry A. *Hermeneutics: Principles and Processes of Biblical Interpretation.* Baker Book House, 1981.

POSTMODERN ISSUES

Kimball, Dan. *Emerging Church: Vintage Christianity for New Generations.* Zondervan, 2003.

McLaren, Brian. *A Generous Orthodoxy.* Zondervan, 2004.

Sweet, Leonard. *Aqua Church: Essential Leadership Arts for Piloting Your Church in Today's Fluid Culture.* Group Publishing, 1999.

Sweet, Leonard. *Soul Tsunami.* Zondervan, 2001.

Sweet, Leonard. *Out of the Question, into the Mystery: Getting Lost in the GodLife Relationship.* Waterbrook Press, 2004.

MISCELLANEOUS ISSUES

Brown, Brene, *Daring Greatly: How the Courage to be Vulnerable Transforms the Way We Live, Love, Parent, and Lead.* Gotham Books, 2012.

Brown, Brene. *The Gifts of Imperfection: Let Go of Who You Think You're Supposed to Be and Embrace Who You Are.* Hazelden Publishing, 2010.

Campbell, Joseph. *The Hero With a Thousand Faces.* Princeton Univ. Press, 1973.

Chesterton, G.K. *The Everlasting Man.* Ignatius Press, 1993.

Copi, Irving M. *Introduction to Logic.* Macmillan Publishing Company, 1982.

Davies, Paul. *The Mind of God: The Scientific Basis for a Rational World.* Simon and Schuster, 1993

Dawson, Raymond, trans. *Confucius: The Analects.* Oxford University Press, 1993

Frankel, Viktor E. *Man's Search for Meaning.* Washington Square Press, 1984

Giles, Herbert A., trans. *Chuang Tzu: Mystic, Moralist, and Social Reformer.* AMS Press, 1974.

Hawking, Stephen. *A Brief History of Time.* Bantam, 1998.

Henricks, Robert G., trans. *Lao Tzu: Te-Tao Ching.* Ballantine Books, 1989.

Merton, Thomas. *The Way of Chuang Tzu.* Shambhala, 2004.

Suzuki, David: *The Sacred Balance: Rediscovering Our Place in Nature,* Greystone Books, 1999

About the Author

David Brisbin, MDiv/LPPC is teaching pastor at theeffect faith community and recovery ministry in San Juan Capistrano, CA. He is also executive director of Encompass Recovery, an addiction treatment center. His twenty five year study of the Hebrew roots of Jesus and Christianity led to his ground level approach to both spiritual formation and substance abuse recovery, processes he sees as one and the same from a practical and contemplative point of view. In addition to guiding people directly at theeffect and remotely through distance learning, his first book, The Fifth Way is available along with several audio series and hundreds of podcasts.

Also by David Brisbin

For more information about David Brisbin, theeffect faith community, spiritual direction, or speaking engagements:

Websites
davebrisbin.com | theeffect.org

Social Media
facebook.com/thedavebrisbin
instagram.com/davebrisbin
twitter.com/davebrisbin
linkedin.com/in/davebrisbin
youtube.com/user/dbrisbin1

Podcasts

Made in the USA
Coppell, TX
31 August 2020

35008928R00146